WORLD BANK TECHNICAL PAPER NO. 491

*World Bank/European Commission
Programme on Private Participation
in Mediterranean Infrastructure*

I0104712

The Development of Electricity Markets in the Euro-Mediterranean Area

*Trends and Prospects for Liberalization
and Regional Integration*

Daniel Müller-Jentsch

*The World Bank
Washington, D.C.*

ISBN: 0-8213-4910-4
ISSN: 0253-7494

Daniel Müller-Jentsch is an economist in the World Bank-European Commission Programme on Private Participation in Mediterranean Infrastructure (Brussels).

Library of Congress Cataloging-in-Publication Data

Müller-Jentsch, Daniel, 1969-
    The development of electricity markets in the Euro-Mediterranean area: trends and prospects for liberalization and regional integration / Daniel Müller-Jentsch.
        p.   cm. — (World Bank technical paper ; no. 491)
    Includes bibliographical references.
    ISBN 0-8213-4910-4
    1. Electric utilities—European Union countries.   2. Electric utilities—Mediterreanean Region.
3. European Union countries—Foreign economic relations—Mediterranean Region. 4. Mediterranean Region—Foreign economic relations—European Union countries.   I. Title. II. Series.

HD9685.E82 M75   2001
333.793′2′094—dc21   00-069317
                                                        CIP

CONTENTS

Diagrams

Boxes

Tables

FOREWORD

This is the first formal publication of the *Programme on Private Participation in Mediterranean Infrastructure* (PPMI), a joint initiative of the World Bank and European Commission. The programme, launched in 1997, assists governments in the Middle East and North Africa in the design and implementation of infrastructure reform, with a particular emphasis on the introduction of competition and regulation. Based in Brussels, PPMI carries out research, provides technical assistance to governments, and helps its sponsoring institutions prepare projects to modernize the legal, regulatory, and institutional framework of infrastructure sectors throughout the region.

Recent PPMI activities in the energy sector include:

- Contribution to the design of three regional Meda energy projects for sector reform, utility restructuring, and support to the ad hoc groups of the Euro-Mediterranean Energy Forum.

- Preparation of the Euro-Mediterranean Energy Forum in Granada (May 2000) on energy policy and sector reform, including submission of a first draft of this report.

- Restructuring of a national Meda project in Lebanon, including the component on electricity reform and two cross-sectoral components on privatization and concessions, as well as review of a national (EC-sponsored) study on energy reform. In all cases, close coordination with ongoing World Bank projects was ensured.

- An in-depth study on the introduction of competition in the Moroccan power sector for the World Bank.

The energy sector is undergoing a major transition worldwide: competition, restructuring, privatization and regulation are at the core of the current revolution, driven in part by new technological developments and changing attitudes toward utilities. Europe's Mediterranean Partners (MPs) can no longer afford to lag behind. Reform in the EU and elsewhere is increasing the relative price of MPs' energy, hence reducing the global competitiveness of the MPs' industry, agriculture and services. MPs have started to open up their power and gas markets, but the choices made to date may prove not to be the right ones: few MPs have yet introduced competition in their power and gas markets and that is where the main challenge of this decade will lie. The approach followed in the 1990s (independent power plants built under BOT schemes with long term power purchase agreements with the national utility) is not likely to yield results equivalent to what effective competition could bring.

With the regional building-blocks for energy reform now largely in place (regional Meda projects, this regional strategy note, the Energy Forum and its ad hoc groups), future efforts should focus more on the national level. Sector adjustment operations, in particular, could become an effective instrument to support sector reform in the coming years. As demonstrated by successful precedents in other sectors (e.g. financial sector in Tunisia, telecommunications sector in Morocco), these could be co-financed by several donors (including the World Bank, the European Commission, and the African Development Bank).

The main objective of this publication is to map out key policy issues that have to be addressed to successfully implement energy sector reform at the national and the regional level. This document is not meant to reproduce the extensive literature, which already exists on the subject of global energy reform and international best practice (see the Bibliography). By providing an overview of global, European, and Mediterranean reform trends, this publication aims to facilitate the dissemination of best practice.

Pierre Guislain

Manager

Programme on Private Participation
In Mediterranean Infrastructure
World Bank / European Commission

ACKNOWLEDGMENTS

I am grateful to many colleagues for their input and advice. Niels de Terra from Hagler Bailly helped draft the first version for the Euro-Mediterranean Energy Forum held in Granada in May 2000. Several parts of the text and particularly Sections 1.2 and 2.2 still bear his mark. Elena Peresso from Eurelectric gave invaluable inputs and dug out many of the facts and figures that can be found in Chapters 2 and 3. Several sections of the document draw heavily on World Bank Viewpoint case studies (available online at *www.worldbank.org/html/fpd/notes/*) and their authors deserve considerable credit. Further contributions came from colleagues in the World Bank and the European Commission including Samuel O'Brien-Kumi, James Moose, and Kamal Shehadi. My main thanks, however, go to Pierre Guislain, who has acted as my mentor over the past three years and who has guided my thinking on so many of the economic and policy issues discussed in this publication.

The analysis and recommendations made throughout the document do not necessarily represent the views of the World Bank or the European Commission. They are meant to contribute to the ongoing discussions between policy makers, donors, and energy companies in the context of the Euro-Mediterranean Partnership in the Energy Sector.

EXECUTIVE SUMMARY

Global Reform Trends in the Energy Sector (Chapter 1)

Energy markets worldwide are currently in the midst of a fundamental transformation, as a result of technological change and policy reforms. The objectives of these reforms are: to enhance efficiency, to lower costs, to increase customer choice, to mobilize private investment, and to consolidate public finances. The mutually reinforcing policy instruments to achieve these objectives are the introduction of competition (often supported by regulation) and the introduction of private participation. As a large number of developed and developing countries have successfully restructured their electricity and gas markets, an international "best practice" for the design of the legal, regulatory, and institutional sector framework has emerged. It includes:

- the corporatization and restructuring of state-owned energy utilities;
- the separation of regulatory and operational functions, the creation of a coherent regulatory framework, and the establishment of an independent regulator to protect consumer interests and promote competition;
- the vertical unbundling of the electricity industry into generation, transmission, distribution, and trade;
- the introduction of competition in generation and trade and the regulation of monopolistic activities in transmission and distribution;
- the promotion of private participation in investment and management through privatization, concessions, and new entry; and
- the reduction of subsidies and tariff-rebalancing in order to bring prices in line with costs and to reduce market distortions.

Energy Sector Restructuring in the European Union (Chapter 2)

Power markets across the European Union (EU) are currently undergoing dramatic structural change triggered primarily by the European Commission Single Market Directive for Electricity. The directive, which entered into force in February 1999, obliges EU Member States to gradually open their power sectors to competition; to vertically unbundle the sector; and to ensure non-discriminatory access to the transmission network. In practice, the minimum standards set by the European Commission have led to a process of "competitive liberalization" across the EU, as most of the countries are going far beyond the minimum. In parallel, the trend towards privatization is gathering momentum, as an increasing number of EU governments are withdrawing from operational involvement in the sector.

Only one year after the electricity directive became effective, its economic impact had already been dramatic. In Germany, one of the most competitive markets in the EU, prices fell by about 20 percent for households and up to 60 percent for industrial users. European cross-border mergers and acquisitions amounted to more than Euro 20 billion in 1999 alone—more than in any other region of the world. In response to competition and new market opportunities, energy companies are restructuring, cutting costs, and offering improved services to customers. Modern power markets and innovative trading instruments are being developed across the continent and previously segmented national markets with a combined annual turnover of Euro 170 billion are integrating rapidly.

Similar developments are now underway in the market for natural gas. According to the Single Market Directive for Natural Gas, Member States (with the exception of emerging gas market countries Greece and Portugal) had to phase in competition as of August 2000. Like in the case of the electricity directive, most Member States are opening a far greater share of the market to competition than required. The European Commission has estimated that 78 percent of EU gas markets were nominally open when the directive became effective. In the UK and Germany, the sector has been fully liberalized since 1998. Italy, Finland, and Ireland have liberalized 70 percent and seven other countries between 30 and 70 percent.

Energy markets across the EU are expected to be fully liberalized, privatized, and integrated across borders by the time the Euro-Mediterranean free trade area (FTA) is to be completed around 2010. European companies and households will benefit from lower prices, better services, and free choice between alternative providers. European utilities will be highly competitive as a result of cost-cutting and consolidation. The EU Single Market for energy is expected to be the largest in the world, comprising not only the current 15 Member States, but also up to 13 accession countries, with a total of more than 400 million consumers.

Sector Developments and Reform Needs in the Mediterranean Partners (Chapter 3)

Despite some encouraging progress in recent years, most of the Mediterranean Partners (MPs) are still lagging significantly behind reform trends in the EU and other regions. In most southern Mediterranean countries, the power sector is still dominated by vertically integrated and state-owned monopolies. Many of the utilities are in need of corporatization and restructuring. Often, regulatory and operational functions have not been separated and sector policies are de facto set by the operator. Few countries in the region have a transparent regulatory framework and virtually none has a truly independent energy regulator (compared to 12 out of 15 EU countries). The legal framework tends to be outdated and sector institutions largely unreformed. Direct and indirect subsidies are widespread, as are price distortions. Across the region, growing energy demand will require significant investments over the coming decade and put further strains on government budgets, unless private capital can be mobilized. In most of the MPs, poor efficiency indicators at the utility and the sector level (e.g. high costs, system losses, government transfers, and energy use intensity) illustrate the need for sector reform and company restructuring.

In several countries, reforms are now underway. In Jordan, for instance, most of the distribution sector has traditionally been privately owned. A new 1998 sector law provides for the establishment of a regulator and the unbundling of the national utility; a privatization strategy is now being developed. In Egypt, a 1998 sector law created 7 regional generation and distribution companies, contrary to the global trend to unbundle. The planned privatization of these companies was recently put on hold, partly due to investor concern about the unreformed regulatory framework. Egypt has been more successful in mobilizing private investment to create a domestic transmission and distribution network for natural gas. In Lebanon, the government has submitted a draft law to Parliament. It launches the reform of the electricity sector by setting up an autonomous regulator and by allowing the unbundling of the national Electricité du Liban. In many countries, including Egypt, Morocco, Tunisia, Turkey, Israel and Jordan, independent power plants (IPPs) are being introduced through international competitive tenders. Several of the MPs have declared their intention to further liberalize and privatize the industry. As EU accession candidates, Turkey, Cyprus, and Malta have started to adopt EU rules.

Despite recent progress, the main structural flaw of energy reform in the region has been the lack of liberalization and effective regulation. While most countries are trying to mobilize private investment for new generation capacity through IPPs, the introduction of competition and more effective regulation are conspicuously absent. This contrasts sharply with reforms in Latin America and even more with those in the EU, where the main focus of the Commission's Single Market Directives for electricity and gas has been the introduction of competition. This lop-sidedness of reforms in the MPs is a cause of concern, since the most important benefits of sector reform are derived from liberalization and not from the privatization of monopolies. As the recent IPP-crisis in Asia has shown, the introduction of IPPs without competition or prior to the modernization of the regulatory framework, can be costly for both the government and the economy at large.

An Agenda for Change: National Reforms and Euro-Med Initiatives (Chapter 4)

On balance, the MPs have taken some important first steps towards sector restructuring. But much remains to be done to modernize their energy sector frameworks. Two decades of global sector reform allow the region to benefit from the international best practice that has emerged. A range of complementary initiatives could help to accelerate sector restructuring and the dissemination of best practice across the southern Mediterranean region:

- Three regional Meda energy projects, to be launched in late 2000, should provide significant analysis and technical assistance (TA) for sector reforms at the policy and the company level.

- Until the meeting in Granada in May 2000, energy policy reform featured only marginally in the discussions of the Energy Forum. At the Granada Forum a consensus emerged that the imminent launch of the three regional projects, together with that of the Ad-Hoc Groups on Energy Policy, Economic Analysis, and Interconnection should be used to give such discussions more prominence.

- National energy projects and sectoral adjustment operations could be used to assist individual countries in sector reform by providing in-depth TA and financial support. For this, however, more active participation of governments in project preparation and implementation would be needed. In the past five years, only Lebanon requested Meda assistance in energy sector policy.

- The planned completion of the Mediterranean Electricity Ring over the coming years could provide the opportunity to create more integrated and competitive cross-border power markets. A fourth regional Meda project on the Mediterranean Ring and the Ad-Hoc Group on Interconnection should be used to explore the regulatory and policy implication of interconnection, as well as the potential for the creation of regional power markets.

The general reform needs in the region are clear. International experience and best practice are there to be tapped. The policy instruments to support comprehensive reforms are available. And the window of opportunity to do so before the implementation of the Euro-Mediterranean FTA is closing fast. It is now up to the MPs and the donor community to tackle the reform agenda.

Chapter 1

INTRODUCTION

1   INTRODUCTION

1.1   The Euro-Mediterranean Partnership and Economic Adjustment

The aim of the Euro-Mediterranean Partnership between the 15 EU member states and their 12 Mediterranean Partners (MPs) is to establish a region of peace and prosperity around the Mediterranean sea.[1] In 1997, the EU had a population of 368 million and the MPs a total of 223 million. Nominal GNP figures were $ 8.6 trillion and $ 0.6 trillion, respectively. In 1998, the EU exported a total of Euro 64 billion to the MPs, while it imported Euro 36 billion.[2] The cornerstones of the Partnership are bilateral Association Agreements between the EU and each of the MPs; a multilateral free-trade area (FTA) to be completed around 2010; and financial assistance in support of social and economic adjustment under the Meda budget line, administered by the European Commission (EC).[3] The Partnership was launched in 1995 at the Barcelona Conference and the various initiatives under the Euro-Med umbrella are being referred to as the Barcelona Process.

The Maghreb and Mashrek countries are becoming increasingly sidelined in the global economy and significant reform efforts will be needed to reverse that trend. The share of the Middle East and North Africa (even including the wealthy Gulf countries) of world trade is a mere 2.5 percent while its share in global foreign direct investment (FDI) is stagnating at 1 percent. During 1995-97, the total net inflow of FDI was equivalent to "0.1 percent of GDP, compared with an average of 2.0 percent for all developing countries [20 times as much], and was the lowest among all regions." The share of Egypt, the largest of these countries, in world exports, for example, fell from an already low 0.17 percent in 1983-86 to 0.07 percent in 1993-96, whereas that of much smaller Chile rose from 0.21 to 0.28 percent during the same period.[4] Other important social and economic indicators are equally alarming.

The average per capita income in the MPs is only one tenth of that in the EU and the Commission estimates that even under an unrealistically optimistic growth scenario, it would

---

[1] The group of MPs includes the *Maghreb* (Morocco, Algeria, and Tunisia); the *Mashrek* (Jordan, Lebanon, Syria, Egypt, and West Bank & Gaza); the three EU accession candidates Turkey (which already has a customs union with the EU), Cyprus, and Malta; as well as Israel. Libya might join in due course.

[2] Population and GDP figures: World Bank, "World Development Indicators 1999". Trade figures: Eurostat. The sub-totals for the eight Maghreb and Mashrek economies are: a GNP of $ 222 billion, a population of 152 million, Euro 49 billion of imports from the EU, and Euro 24 billion of exports to the EU.

[3] Since EU accession will require more comprehensive reforms by Cyprus, Malta and Turkey, and since Turkey already has a customs union with the EU, these three countries are not signing Euro-Med *Association Agreements* (AAs). The AAs, in which both sides primarily commit themselves to gradual trade liberalization, have already entered into force in the case of Tunisia, Morocco, Israel, and WB&G (an interim agreement). The AA for Jordan has been signed but ratification is pending; the one for Egypt has been concluded but is awaiting signature; and Algeria, Lebanon, and Syria are in relatively early stages of negotiations. The *Meda budget line* provides grant money for projects and programs in the magnitude of about Euro 1 billion per year, complemented by loans of similar magnitude by the European Investment Bank (EIB). 90 percent of Meda money is earmarked for national projects in the eight Maghreb and Mashrek MPs, while the remaining 10 percent fund regional projects.

[4] World Bank Institute / Mediterranean Development Forum, "Trade Policy Developments in the Middle East and North Africa" (2000). Quote from Chapter 1 by M. Nabli and A. De Kleine; figures from Chapter 5 by A. Refaat. Another indicator for trade openness cited, paints the same picture: While Egypt's trade to GDP ratio fell from 32 to 25 percent in that period, Chile's grew from 44 to 48.

take 40 years to just halve this income gap.[5] According to John Page, former World Bank chief economist for the MENA region, "MENA is becoming increasingly marginalized as the globalization of goods and capital markets accelerates. While other developing economies are successfully advancing on a ladder of dynamic comparative advantage, towards human capital and technology-intensive goods, the MENA region risks becoming increasingly specialized in energy exports and labor intensive, low-skilled manufactures."[6]

The Euro-Med free-trade area provides an opportunity for economic growth, which the Maghreb and Mashrek countries must seize. Even though the FTA does not cover all economic sectors (e.g. agriculture and services are so far excluded), the direct and indirect gains from trade could become a key driver of social and economic development throughout the southern Mediterranean. For this to happen, however, these countries will have to comprehensively modernize their economic and social structures in order to prepare their industry for the competition and opportunities associated with the FTA. As the example of the North American Free Trade Area (NAFTA) and more than a decade of radical economic reform in Mexico have shown, this can be achieved.

The Barcelona Declaration, the founding document of the Euro-Mediterranean Partnership reflects these realities. It states that "the participants decided to facilitate the progressive establishment of this free-trade area through … the pursuit and the development of policies based on the principles of market economy and the integration of their economies (…); the adjustment and modernization of their economic and social structures, giving priority to the promotion and development of the private sector (…) and to the establishment of an appropriate institutional and regulatory framework for a market economy." It also stresses "the importance of creating an environment conducive to investment" and acknowledges "the pivotal role of the energy sector in the economic Euro-Mediterranean partnership." One of the main instruments for the implementation of this strategy is the Meda budget line ("Mesures d'Accompagnement"), which funds national and regional projects in support of economic adjustment.

Energy and particularly electricity sector reform should be an integral part of all national programs for economic adjustment. The electricity sector is not only important in its own right (it constitutes a significant part of GDP and national investment) but also an important input for other industries. Increasing the efficiency of the sector through more competition and better regulation, will help to increase economic growth and employment. The privatization of power utilities would mobilize much-needed foreign direct investment (FDI), reduce public debt, and free government resources for more important priorities like education or rural development. Moreover, it will bring private sector management and innovation to the sector. The increase of tariffs to cost-recovery levels and the reduction of public subsidies will reduce wasteful overconsumption and increase energy efficiency, thus benefiting the environment. The same applies to the natural gas and oil sectors. Since only a few of the MPs have significant hydrocarbon reserves, however, and since the region is only now starting to create downstream markets for natural gas, the main emphasis of this publication is on the electricity market.

---

[5] This is under the assumption that annual per capita growth is 5 percent in the MPs and 1 percent in the EU.

[6] From the Mediterranean Development Forum in Marrakech (September 1998). The Middle East and North Africa (MENA) region, in the World Bank definition of the term, includes the countries of the Arab peninsula, but excludes Turkey, Cyprus, and Malta.

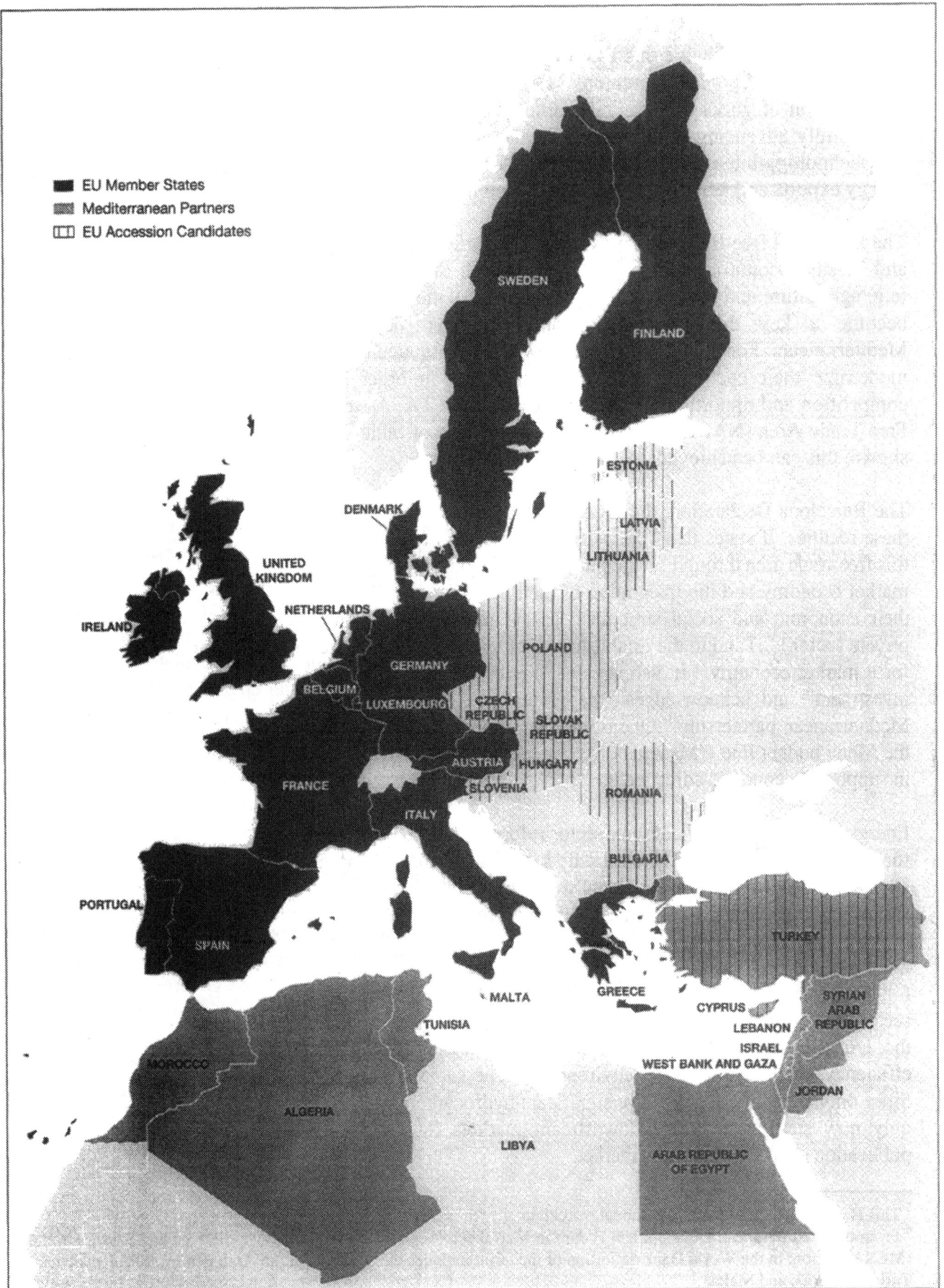

Legend:
- ■ EU Member States
- ▨ Mediterranean Partners
- ⊞ EU Accession Candidates

SWEDEN

FINLAND

ESTONIA

LATVIA

LITHUANIA

DENMARK

UNITED KINGDOM

NETHERLANDS

IRELAND

POLAND

GERMANY

BELGIUM

LUXEMBOURG

CZECH REPUBLIC

SLOVAK REPUBLIC

AUSTRIA

HUNGARY

FRANCE

SLOVENIA

ROMANIA

ITALY

BULGARIA

PORTUGAL

SPAIN

TURKEY

MALTA

GREECE

CYPRUS

SYRIAN ARAB REPUBLIC

LEBANON

TUNISIA

ISRAEL

WEST BANK AND GAZA

MOROCCO

JORDAN

ALGERIA

LIBYA

ARAB REPUBLIC OF EGYPT

1.2   Global Trends in Electricity Sector Policy

The electricity industry has gone through three major phases over the last century, and is now entering a fourth one. Until recently the power sector and other network industries (oil, gas, water and telecommunications) were considered to be "natural monopolies". Due to technological progress and the development of new regulatory instruments, however, the introduction of effective market mechanisms is now possible. The exact evolution of the industry has varied from country to country, but the following pattern in the development of the electricity and downstream gas markets has been observed:

Phase I: Private Sector Investment and Monopolistic Market Behavior

The infrastructure investments in the late 19th century and early 20th century were largely undertaken by private companies. The Middle East and North Africa was no exception. Private firms developed and commercialized the technologies for the production and delivery of electricity and natural gas. Local monopolies, and national and international oligopolies that used their market power to extract economic rents from captive customers, dominated the new industry. Delivery to users was generally confined to urban communities, with limited development of distribution grids in rural areas. There was little competition in the sector during this period of rapid innovation and industry expansion.

Phase II: Public Sector Intervention and Inefficiency

Around the time of World War II, a trend towards the nationalization of energy assets or at least strong government regulation of privately-owned monopolies became the norm, in an attempt to limit abuses of market power. In many countries, governments also played an important role in rural electrification, since returns were too low to attract private capital. Throughout the EU and elsewhere, state-ownership of the electricity industry became the rule. Over time, however, public ownership and the absence of competition increasingly undermined effective management, innovation and operational efficiency. Governments used the power sector, like other state-owned industries, to artificially create employment and as an instrument to deliver hidden subsidies to parts of the economy.

Phase III: Unbundling, Competition, Regulation and Privatization

The economic costs of public ownership and monopolistic market structures became more and more apparent. In the 1970s the United States began to experiment with power sector reform. By the 1980s policy-makers in the EU, the Americas and elsewhere realized that electricity, natural gas and telecommunications were no longer natural monopolies. Thanks to advances in technology, economic theory, and increasingly sophisticated regulatory instruments, it became feasible to introduce competition with the same effect as in other industries. Substantial improvements in operational and investment efficiency, the reduction of costs to end-users, an improvement of services, and a higher rate of innovation thus became possible. During the 1990s, electricity and natural gas sectors have been transformed through the overhaul of regulatory frameworks, the introduction of competition, and increasing private participation. These policy reforms have been implemented in developed and developing countries alike.

Phase IV: Industry Convergence and Globalization

The fourth phase, which is now overlapping with the third, is characterized by convergence in the electricity, natural gas, and more generally the utility sector. "Multi-utilities" are being formed to offer comprehensive service-packages to clients and reap the associated economies of scope. As liberalization and privatization are taking hold, the industry is rapidly globalizing through international mergers and acquisitions, cross-border trade, and the creation of regional power pools. Another facet of the fourth phase is the emergence of a new "service" sector in the power industry, quite distinct from physical distribution, classified now as the "wires" business.

The trends outlined above have been global, but developments have been uneven across regions. North America pioneered reforms in the 1980s, but due to its federal structure has not yet completed the process in all states. Except for the UK and the Nordic countries, Europe embraced reforms relatively late but vigorously so and is now arguably the fastest reforming continent. Latin America, the first developing region to liberalize and privatize its energy sector, has largely completed the reform agenda. Many countries in Asia that introduced IPPs without liberalization, suffered from the consequences during the recent financial crisis, and are now moving toward the Latin American model. Together with Sub-Saharan Africa, the countries of the southern Mediterranean are lagging considerably behind international reform trends. The following two diagrams illustrate the reform progress made by different countries and show how far the MPs (Diagram 2) have fallen behind the rest of the world (Diagram 1).

The two regions, whose developments are of the most significance for the MPs, are arguably Europe and Latin America. Latin America (outlined in Section 1.3) is relevant because the initial conditions prior to reform are similar to the situation in the southern Mediterranean today. Moreover, the countries of Latin America are 10 to 20 years ahead of the MPs in terms of sector reform. They have experimented with different reform models and accumulated a wealth of experience, from which the MPs can benefit. The developments in Europe (analyzed in Chapter 2) are relevant for the southern Mediterranean region due to geographical proximity and the emerging Euro-Mediterranean free-trade area.

Diagram 1: Global Reform Trends in the Power Sector

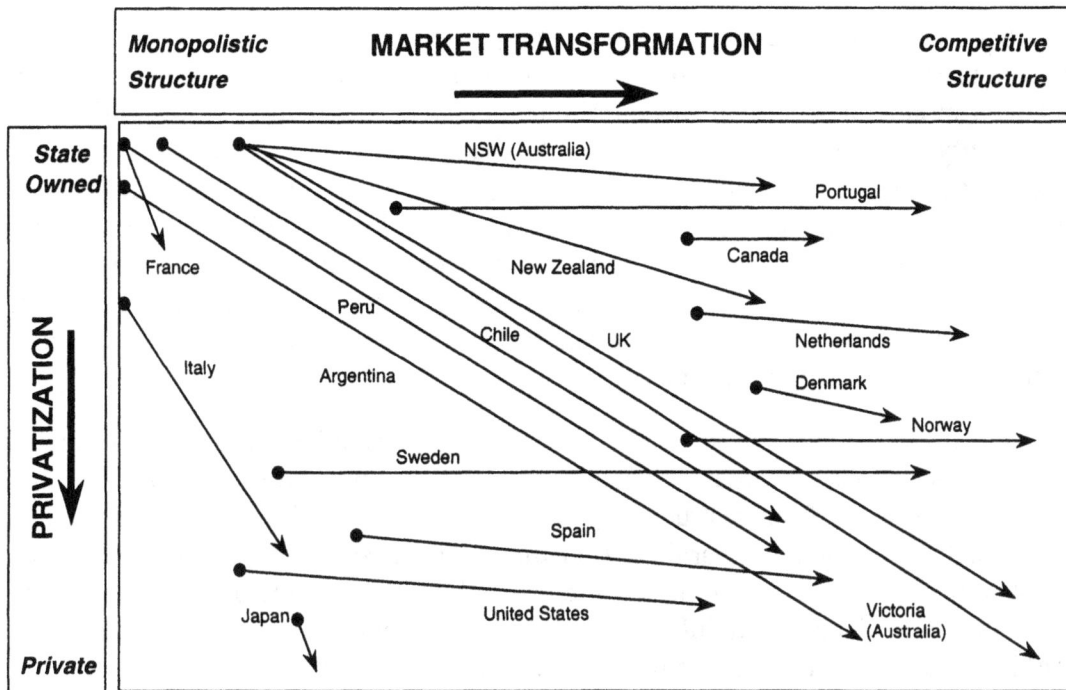

MARKET TRANSFORMATION

Monopolistic Structure — Competitive Structure

State Owned — Private

PRIVATIZATION

NSW (Australia), Portugal, France, New Zealand, Canada, Peru, Chile, UK, Netherlands, Argentina, Italy, Denmark, Norway, Sweden, Spain, Japan, United States, Victoria (Australia)

Source: Hagler Bailly.

Diagram 2: Sector Reform in the Mediterranean Partners

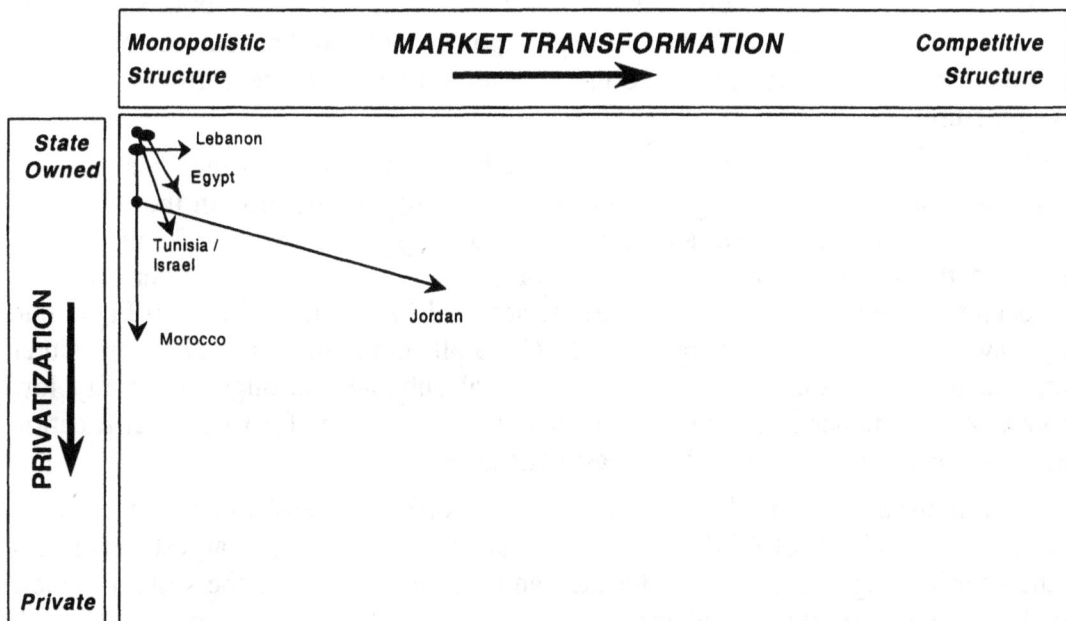

MARKET TRANSFORMATION

Monopolistic Structure — Competitive Structure

State Owned — Private

PRIVATIZATION

Lebanon, Egypt, Tunisia / Israel, Jordan, Morocco

Source: World Bank.

Focusing on the two key policy parameters—the introduction of competition (including regulation) and the introduction of private participation—the arrows in Diagram 1 illustrate the reform progress made by selected countries over the past two decades. Diagram 2 shows selected MPs. Their clustering in the upper left-hand corner and the short extension of their arrows illustrate the urgency to catch up.

7

1.3   The South American Reform Experience

The South American experience may hold some particularly relevant policy lessons for the MPs. First, the market structure prior to reforms and thus the reform challenges are similar: vertically integrated monopolies, state-ownership, underdeveloped regulatory frameworks, low efficiency at the utility-level, and political resistance to change. Second, other initial conditions are also comparable: the state of economic development, the need to reduce the fiscal burden imposed by the sector, high demand growth, the coexistence of both small and large systems within the region, and the potential for sub-regional power pools. Third, since Latin American energy reforms started in the 1980s and since different countries experimented with alternative reform models, the Mediterranean countries can benefit from a large pool of policy experience and best practice that has emerged in the process:[7]

- *Unbundling and Competition:* As the reform pioneer, Chile privatized without introducing pro-competitive restrictions on cross-ownership and market concentration. Consequently, few of the efficiency gains from restructuring under private ownership were passed on to consumers through lower prices. Learning from this mistake, subsequent reformers in the region like Argentina, Peru, Bolivia, and Columbia unbundled the sector into generation, dispatch, transmission, distribution infrastructure, and distribution supply. Argentina, for instance, sold generation capacity to competing private companies and prohibits generators to own more than 10 percent of total capacity. Distribution is separated into "wires" (the physical network as a natural monopoly) and sales (the service of delivering power through the network, which is potentially competitive). For larger users, regulatory rules for third-party access permit competition in distribution. For small retail customers, both supply and wires are regulated to prevent the abuse of monopoly power by local distribution companies. In most South American countries entry into the generation market is free, further increasing competitive pressure.

- *Tariffs and Subsidies:* Another component of the "Southern Cone model" which has emerged is the deregulation of prices, including the introduction of full competition in the wholesale market (i.e. sales from generators and importers to large customers and distribution companies), and the regulation of retail prices for smaller consumers. Another common feature has been the elimination of subsidies to the sector. In Argentina, the 1989 Economic Emergency Law suspended all such transfers. In Chile all remaining subsidies were either closely targeted to low income groups (i.e. no general subsidies through artificially low prices) or awarded on the basis of competitive tenders (e.g. subsidies for rural electrification went to those companies that demanded the least assistance).

- *Dispatch:* The rule used for dispatch is the one of "merit-order", whereby cheapest power is dispatched first. A drawback of Chile's system management is that the largest generators dominate the coordinating committee for dispatch and can thus influence the system to their advantage. In contrast, Argentina and other countries opted for an independent dispatch entity and thus for full unbundling.

- *Regulation:* As far as price regulation is concerned, different mechanisms are being used in the monopolistic activities of transmission and distribution. Chile, for instance, uses a

---

[7] Much of the information in this section is taken from "Key Issues and Lessons Learned from Electricity Sector Reforms in Latin America", prepared for the IDB and USAID by Hagler Bailly Services (1999).

hypothetical "model utility" as a benchmark to determine the adequate rate of return and thereby the fair price. Argentina uses price-cap regulation. In-between periodic price adjustment, cost reductions resulting from productivity increases are shared between investors and consumers to strike a balance between the need to provide an incentive for cost reductions and the desire to see them passed on to end-users. In all Latin American countries, regulation has played a critical role in increasing competition and efficiency. Most of the countries have established an independent regulator.

- *Privatization:* Most Latin American countries have either completed or at least launched the privatization of assets in the electricity market. As Diagram 6 in Section 3.1 shows, Latin America has attracted a total of about $ 80 billion of private investment into the power sector —the highest of all developing regions. Diagram 3 below gives the breakdown of these figures over the past decade. An important feature of the investment pattern is the high percentage of actual privatizations (divestitures), as opposed to greenfield projects. This contrasts sharply with the situation in the southern Mediterranean, where governments are still reluctant to sell energy assets and privatization is confined to IPPs.

Diagram 3: Annual Private Investments in Latin American Power (1990–99)

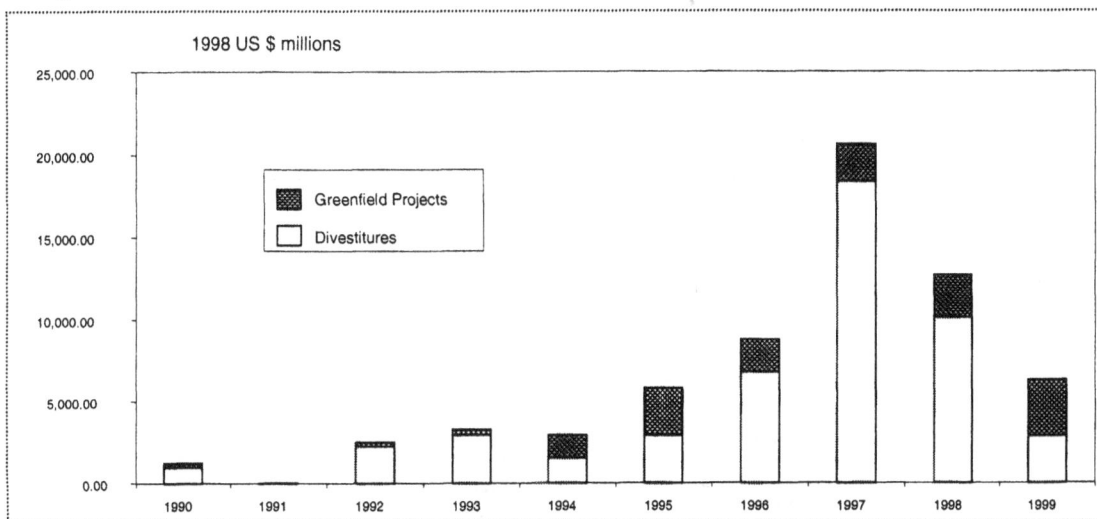

Source: World Bank.

The economic and social benefits South America derived from energy sector reform are illustrated by performance indicators for the Argentinean power sector. Between 1992 and 1997 average spot price nearly halved from 42 to 25 $/MWh, thermal availability increased from 48 to 75 percent, and distribution losses were reduced from 21 to 12 percent. When private operators took over retail supply in Buenos Aires, losses amounted to $ 150 million in the 16 months following privatization. After a systematic reduction of power theft and efficiency increases, losses were reduced from 30 to 12 percent, and the company generated a profit of $ 50 million in 1995. Increased productivity among the privatized generators was associated with substantial layoffs (up to 40 percent of staff), whose social effects were minimized through retraining and severance payments. Despite such transition costs, overall economic gains derived from power sector reform are estimated to amount to $ 2.3 billion, close to one percent of Argentina's GDP.[9]

---

[9] "Winners and Losers from the Privatization and Regulation of Utilities: Lessons from a General Equilibrium

1.4 A Check List: Best Practice in Electricity Sector Reform

The international best practice for the modernization of the legal, regulatory, and institutional framework in the electricity sector is summarized in the policy check-list below. Please refer to the Bibliography at the end of the document for further reading.

Unbundling and Competition

- Unbundle vertically integrated monopolies to separate natural monopoly elements (i.e. transmission and distribution) from market segments where competition is feasible (i.e. generation, trade).
- Liberalize potentially competitive market segments by subdividing former monopolies in generation (into competing entities) and distribution (into regional monopolies). Create open and transparent markets for energy (solid and liquid fuels, gas and electricity).
- Shift the role of the state from asset ownership and operation to sector policy and regulation ("from player to referee").
- Pursue social and environmental objectives using policy instruments that are transparent, well targeted, and minimize market distortions.

Regulation

- Fully separate operational and regulatory functions.
- Use sector regulation and general competition policy to prevent anti-competitive behavior by utilities and to protect consumer interests.
- Create a clear, transparent, and accountable regulatory framework.
- Ensure full autonomy, financial viability, technical expertise, and transparency of regulatory bodies.

Tariffs and Subsidies

- Rebalance prices to ensure they reflect true economic costs and promote efficiency.
- Where possible, let competitive markets set prices. Regulate prices where they are distorted by monopolistic structures and in cases of market failure.
- Strengthen discipline in the collection of payments and eliminate power theft.
- Gradually eliminate production and investment subsidies and close uneconomic facilities (e.g. coal mines, refineries, power plants).

Private Participation

- Private energy companies, and not the government, should be responsible for the planning and financing of investments, as well as the management of utilities.
- Do not introduce private participation- before competition and regulatory reform. Governments facing fiscal constraints should resist the temptation to introduce IPPs before adopting a clear energy policy and before modernizing the legal and regulatory framework.
- Encourage the inflow of know-how and foreign direct investment to the energy sector by providing an efficient and transparent regulatory framework.

Model of Argentina" by Chisari, Estache, and Romero; World Bank Economic Review (May 1999)

- Consider accession to the Energy Charter Treaty to improve the investment climate.

Company Restructuring
- Commercialize and corporatize state-owned utilities.
- Unbundle generation, distribution, and transmission/dispatch (i.e. separation of accounts, division of assets, creation of separate organizational entities).
- Restructure utility companies to render them more efficient (e.g. cost-cutting, financial restructuring, commercial management).
- Privatize generation and distribution companies *after* unbundling and reforming the regulatory framework.
- Involve foreign strategic investors in the restructuring process.

Energy Trade and Cross-border Issues
- Open domestic energy markets to international competition, especially in the case of countries with small systems.
- Eliminate remaining export taxes on fuels and electricity.
- Strengthen the institutional and regulatory framework for energy trade.
- Facilitate the construction of transnational oil and gas pipelines, as well as power grid interconnections.
- Improve the availability and quality of sector statistics, exchange information, and carry out regional benchmarking exercises, to disseminate best practice and coordinate reforms across the region.

Social Protection
- Assist energy companies with the process of shedding surplus staff in a socially acceptable manner (e.g. re-training, early retirement, severance payments).
- Support the poor through targeted and means-tested direct subsidies, instead of general price subsidies, in order to reduce the costs and distortions caused by such interventions.
- In countries with a low rate of rural electrification, subsidize rural infrastructure investment but maximize private participation and use tenders to minimize cost.

Environmental Protection
- Raise tariffs to cost-recovery levels and phase out subsidies to reduce wasteful overconsumption of energy.
- Restructure and privatize utilities to reduce system losses, increase energy efficiency, and facilitate investments in new technology.
- Enforce emission standards (e.g. requirement to use fuels with low sulfur and lead content) and levy pollution taxes proportionate to the environmental costs of different fuels and technologies ("polluter-pays" principle).
- Facilitate market entry of environmentally friendly technologies.

Sequencing of Reform and Consensus Building

- Due to complex interdependencies between the various reform measures listed above, poorly prepared or sub-optimally sequenced reforms can be ineffective or even counterproductive. The introduction of private participation (e.g. IPPs, privatization) prior to the introduction of competition and the overhaul of the regulatory framework, for instance, can lead to private monopolies and considerably reduce the scope for future reforms ("policy lock-in").
- Even though the economic benefits of well-prepared reform clearly outweigh their costs, they are often prevented by vested interest groups or political fear of transition costs (e.g. staff reductions, tariff adjustments). Consensus building and public communication about the benefits of reforms are needed to overcome such obstacles.

As outlined in the Introduction, the southern Mediterranean countries are lagging behind the EU and developing regions both in terms of overall economic performance (Section 1.1) and in terms of energy sector reform (Sections 1.2 and 1.3). Despite recent reform efforts, these gaps are still growing. The Euro-Mediterranean free-trade area not only increases the need but also provides a unique opportunity for broad economic adjustment and far-reaching energy sector restructuring. The Mediterranean Partners should seize this opportunity. They can learn from the reform experience of other countries in order to catch up and possibly even leapfrog those who reformed before them.

Chapter 2

Power Sector Reform in the European Union

2   POWER SECTOR REFORM IN THE EUROPEAN UNION

2.1   Introduction

With a combined annual turnover of about Euro 170 billion, investments of more than Euro 25 billion per year, and an installed capacity of 641 GW, the power sector is one of the largest sectors in EU Single Market.[9] One of the most important economic measures taken by the European Union (EU) in recent years, was the creation of a single market for electricity and gas, based on the principles of transparent regulation and open competition. An important factor behind the decision to liberalize this market was the realization that EU companies were paying up to 40 percent more for electricity and gas than their competitors in the USA and Australia. If energy-intensive industries in the EU were to remain competitive in the global economy, energy costs had to be brought down through increased efficiency and more dynamic competition.

The Single Market Directive for Electricity, which has triggered an unexpectedly rapid and far-reaching restructuring of EU power markets, entered into force in February 1999.[10] Its main provisions and the status of implementation by Member States is outlined in Section 2.2. The remaining Sections of this chapter will describe other facets of the industry's metamorphosis, namely the development of regulatory institutions (Section 2.3); the emergence of power markets and trading instruments (Section 2.4); the restructuring of power utilities (Section 2.5); as well as cross-border integration of electricity markets and sector reform in the accession countries of Eastern and Central Europe (Section 2.6). The Commission's approach to electricity liberalization has been to define a common set of regulatory principles, while leaving their detailed implementation to individual EU governments and the resolution of many technical issues to industry participants. In practice, the minimum standards set by the European Commission (EC) have led to a process of "competitive liberalization", as most countries have already fully liberalized their power markets or are committed to go far beyond the minimum standards set by the EC.

In early 2000, only one year after the Internal Electricity Market Directive became effective, its economic impact had already been significant. Throughout the EU, competition is eroding monopoly rents and lowering electricity prices for consumers. This trend is illustrated by Diagram 4, which shows price reductions in the individual Member States between 1996 and 1999.[11] In most countries, prices have fallen further since, even though rising oil prices could reverse that trend. At the beginning of 2000, prices in Germany, for instance, had fallen by about 20 percent for households and up to 60 percent for industrial users. As utilities are restructuring rapidly to save costs and compete, consolidation within national markets and across borders is accelerating. In 1999

---

[9] EURELECTRIC (see section 2.5) maintains a statistical database for the sector, called EURPROG. For 1997, it recorded (i) a turnover of Euro 163 billion; (ii) investments of Euro 26 billion; (iii) 193 million consumers; (iv) consumption of 2282 TWh; (v) and net generation capacity of 641 GW.

[10] The directive formally entered into force on 19 February 1997, but the deadline for its implementation was two years later (19 February 1999). Six years of tough political negotiations were needed before the directive could be agreed upon, due to the reluctance of some EU Member States to liberalize their power sector.

[11] The UK, which experienced price rises, is a notable exception since it was the first EU country to fully liberalize its power markets. Prices had already been among the lowest in the EU.

alone, cross-border mergers and acquisitions (M&As) amounted to more than Euro 20 billion—making Europe the most important market for energy M&As worldwide.[13]

Diagram 4: Price Reductions in EU Countries (1996–99, cumulative)

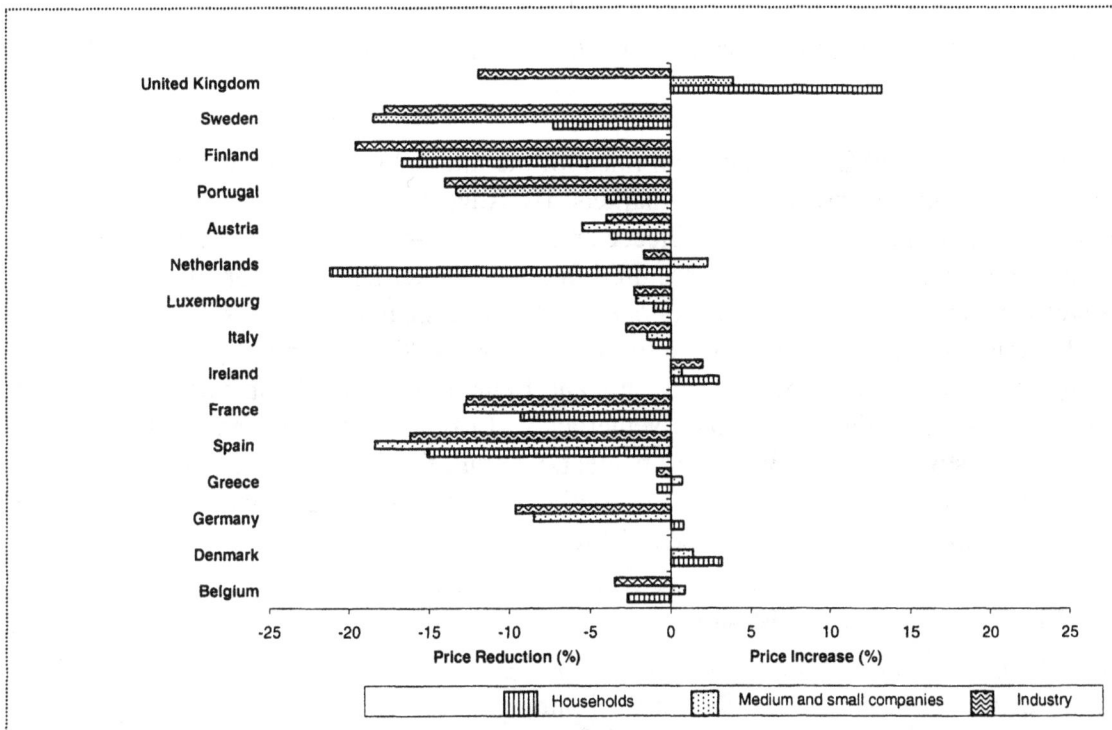

Source: EURELECTRIC.

In the UK, the EU country that pioneered energy sector liberalization and privatization in the 1980s, the impact of reforms on efficiency and prices has been well documented. Following the launch of electricity privatization in 1991, "manning in the transmission network [was] cut by a third, and by half in local distribution systems. Prices to industrial consumers have fallen by up to a third in real terms since privatization. Tariffs for domestic consumers had fallen by a quarter by April 1999. And further cuts of up to 15 percent are in prospect."[14] In the gas sector, "industrial gas prices fell by over 40 percent in real terms [adjusting for inflation] between 1992 and 1996 during a period of intense competition, when the former monopoly supplier's industrial market share was cut to around 25 percent [...] In 1990 UK industrial gas prices were the seventh lowest in the EU, but by 1996 were the lowest."[15] Other economic benefits of reform included several billion Euro worth of privatization receipts and taxes which the government now collects from private utilities.

In addition to liberalization, the privatization of power utilities across the EU is far advanced. The Commission has no mandate to force EU Member States to privatize state assets. However, the fact that the industry is increasingly being driven by market forces, combined with a general

---

[13] Financial Times (8 December 1999)

[14] Financial Times (26 November 1999)

[15] "The Social Effects of Energy Liberalization – The UK Experience", UK Department of Trade and Industry (May 2000)

15

privatization trend across the EU, has convinced most Member States that it is time to phase out public ownership in the sector. In the UK, for instance, the privatization of power and gas markets was completed in 1990. The Portuguese government privatized the first 30 percent of the public power utility EdP in 1997 and another 20 percent for $ 2 billion in October 2000. Many German municipalities (including the capital Berlin) have already sold or are planning to sell their stakes in energy utilities. The privatization of 34.5 percent of the Italian power utility Enel in late 1999 generated Euro 18 billion for the treasury and was the world's largest ever initial public offering (IPO).

Thanks to the Directive 98/30/EC on "common rules for the internal market in natural gas", similar developments are now under way in EU gas markets. By August 2000, Member States—with the exception of emerging gas market countries Greece and Portugal—were obliged to start liberalizing the sector. As in the case of the similarly structured Internal Market Directive for Electricity, most Member States are planning to or have already opened a greater share of the market to competition than required (a minimum of 33 percent over a ten-year period). In the UK and Germany, the sector has been fully liberalized since 1998. Italy, Finland, and Ireland have already opened 70 percent of their gas markets. In Austria, Spain, the Netherlands, Luxembourg, Sweden, Belgium, and Denmark, this figure stood between 30 and 70 percent. Overall, the Commission estimated that 78 percent of the EU market for natural gas were nominally open by the due date, even though a number of important technical issues remained to be resolved.[15]

Box 1: EU Institutions and EU Legislation

The *European Union* (EU) is a *supranational organization*, i.e. its 15 Member States have partly ceded national sovereignty to multilateral EU institutions. The *European Commission* (EC), as the executive branch of the EU, prepares EU legislation in the form of *regulations* (legally binding upon their entry into force) and *directives* (general principles to be transposed into national law by Member States). It also manages the EU's Euro 90 billion per year budget, approximately 10 percent of which go to external programs. The *MEDA program* for the southern Mediterranean countries, about Euro 1 billion of grant money annually, is primarily managed by the Directorate General for External Relations (*DG Relex*) and the *Common Service* (project implementation unit for all regions outside the EU, to be renamed *Europe Aid* in early 2001). These funds are complemented by a similar amount of loans from the *European Investment Bank* (EIB), the EU's long-term financing institution. The Directorate General for Transport and Energy (*DG TREN*) is playing a leading role in the liberalization of EU energy markets and holds the secretariat of the Euro-Mediterranean Energy Partnership.

The EC is politically controlled by the *Council of Ministers* (representatives of Member State governments) and increasingly by the *European Parliament* (directly elected representatives). The corpus of EU law is referred to as the *acquis communautaire*. Important economic legislation includes the comprehensive regulatory framework for the *EU Single Market* as well as *competition and state aid rules*, where the Commission also has comprehensive investigating and enforcement powers. For the energy sector, the two most important pieces of legislation have been the Internal Market Directive for Electricity and the Internal Market Directive for Gas (see text for details). Cross-sectoral competition policy also plays an important role (see Box 2). Legislative documents, as well as additional background information can be downloaded from the EU web-site (*www.europa.eu.int*).

---

[15] Technical obstacles to effective competition included network access, interoperability, balancing regimes, capacity constraints, and transmission tariffs. Information from Oxford Analytica Brief (12 July 2000) and DG

By the time the Euro-Mediterranean free-trade area (FTA) is to be completed around 2010, energy markets across the EU are likely to be fully liberalized, largely privatized, and closely integrated across borders. Companies and households will benefit from low prices, better services, and free choice between providers. The single market for energy is likely not only to include the current 15 Member States but also up to 13 accession countries of Central and Eastern Europe and the Mediterranean region (see Section 2.6). These have started to adopt EU rules in the energy sector, as one of the preconditions for accession. As enlargement candidates, the three MPs Turkey, Cyprus, and Malta are already part of that process. The Maghreb and Mashrek countries should consider similar reforms if they want to maintain the competitiveness of their economies and prepare their energy companies for the competition and opportunities that will arise within the FTA.

2.2   **Liberalization**

The Commission's Internal Electricity Market Directive (96/92/EC), which became effective on 19 February 1999, was a watershed for the liberalization of power markets across the EU. It stipulates that EU Member States have to (i) gradually open up their power sectors to competition from a minimum of 25 percent in 1999 to 33 percent by 2003; (ii) vertically unbundle the sector for the sake of increased competition and transparency; (iii) grant indiscriminate access to the transmission network; and (iv) ensure that market participants comply with technical standards to allow for interoperability (a precondition for effective market integration and competition).

Phased Introduction of Competition

For a market to be truly competitive, consumers need the freedom to purchase electricity from the supplier of their choice. The directive sets minimum requirements concerning the percentage of the market where such choice is possible. The Directive requires Member State governments to progressively open national markets in three stages: 26 percent by February 1999, 28 percent by 2000 and 33 percent by 2003. Belgium and Ireland were granted a one-year extension (which Belgium did not use), and Greece a two-year extension. The rationale for the gradual introduction of competition was to give industry participants enough time for internal restructuring and the establishment of new trading systems.

Most EU countries decided to go far beyond these minimum standards. According to the Commission, around 60 percent of the EU electricity market had formally been opened by May 2000. As shown in Diagram 5, the UK, Germany, Sweden and Finland have already opened 100 percent of their markets. Denmark, by permitting all distributors to purchase freely, is indirectly opening up 90 percent of its electricity market by the end of 2000 and 100 percent by 2002. In Austria, complete liberalization is scheduled for 2001, in Holland for 2003, in Spain for 2004, and in Belgium for 2010. Some countries are expected to bring these dates further forward.

TREN, "State of Implementation of the EU Gas Directive" (May 2000)

Diagram 5: Market Opening in Individual EU Member States

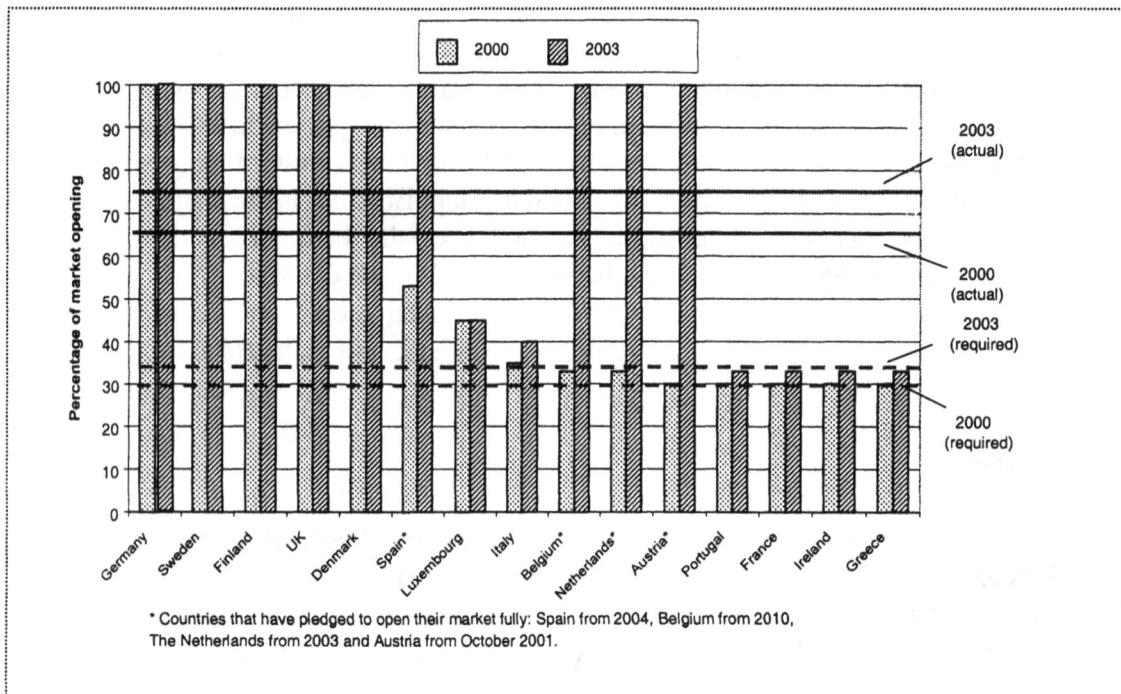

Legend: 2000, 2003

Y-axis: Percentage of market opening

X-axis: Germany, Sweden, Finland, UK, Denmark, Spain*, Luxembourg, Italy, Belgium*, Netherlands*, Austria*, Portugal, France, Ireland, Greece

Reference lines: 2003 (actual); 2000 (actual); 2003 (required); 2000 (required)

* Countries that have pledged to open their market fully: Spain from 2004, Belgium from 2010, The Netherlands from 2003 and Austria from October 2001.

Source: EURELECTRIC.

Another prerequisite for the ability of consumers to shop around (besides the formal freedom to do so), however, is the existence of a sufficient number of generation companies. The exact number of generators needed for effective competition, however, depends on the circumstances (e.g. size of market, quality of regulation, competition from abroad). The electricity directive does not provide guidelines for the horizontal unbundling of generation and EU governments use different policies to tackle this issue:

- In *Italy*, the former state monopoly Enel is legally obliged to reduce its market share by selling power plants with a total generation capacity of 15,000 MW (a third of its total) to competitors.[16] Decree 79/1999 stipulates that after 2002, no company will be allowed to directly or indirectly produce or import more than 50 percent of the country's electricity. In July 2000, the power producers Edison and Sondel announced a merger and their intention to purchase some of Enel's assets in order to position themselves as the third largest generator.

- In *Germany* generation has traditionally been more fragmented, but two large mergers between RWE/VEW and Veba/Viag threatened to create a duopoly. To prevent this, both national and EU competition authorities cooperated closely to impose strict conditionalities in return for their approval in mid-2000. Both groups will shed all cross-shareholdings to reduce the risk of collusion. In particular, they will sell their respective shares in east German VEAG and thus create an independent third force in the market (the fourth one being Energy Baden-Württemberg). Moreover, rules governing transmission will be modified substantially to reduce the ability of both groups to stifle competition through their control over the

---

[16] For that purpose, Enel has transferred power plants to three new subsidiaries, which are to be sold: Eurogen (7,008 MW), Elettrogen (5,438 MW), and Interpower (2,611 MW).

transmission network. Veba has also agreed to free capacity in the Denmark interconnector to allow for additional cross-border competition through increased imports from Scandinavia.[18]

- *Spain* is another country that uses competition policy to restrict market power in generation. In June 2000, the authorities vetoed a merger between Union Fenosa and Hidroelectrica de Cantabrico, which would have reduced the number of generation companies from four to three.

- Finally, cross-border trade and competition is eroding the market dominance of incumbent generators across the EU—even in countries with a high degree of market concentration. In *Belgium*, for example, the German utility RWE is undermining Tractebel's monopoly by serving large industrial customers, including Ford's Genk car factory and BASF's chemical plant in Antwerp.[19]

Both in terms of market opening and horizontal unbundling of generation, EU Member States have liberalized much faster than expected. A number of forces are driving the process of "competitive liberalization" between them. First, industrial users and consumers are exerting public pressure by demanding lower prices and better services. Second, the visible economic benefits reaped by those countries that have already reformed, are inducing governments of more hesitant countries to accelerate liberalization. Finally, policy makers are trying to prepare their energy companies for competition in the EU Single Market by exposing them to greater competition in their domestic market. In many cases, the entrenched position of the incumbent as well as technical and legal teething problems are still limiting competition in practice. According to most industry observers, however, EU energy markets are likely to be largely liberalized over the next five years.

At the European Council in Lisbon (24 March 2000), Member States asked the European Commission to come up with proposals to further accelerate the liberalization of the electricity and gas markets by mid-2001. Two key concerns are the full separation in all Member States between transmission and generation, as well as the guarantee of non-discriminatory third-party access. Apart from these considerations, the Commission has been invited to look into other issues affecting the functioning of the market, notably cross-border transmission pricing and an effective congestion management system. These two issues lie at the core of the Florence Process (see Box 4). A similar initiative now exists for gas and is referred to as the Madrid Process. In a recent report, the European Parliament supports the conclusions of the European Council and requests the Commission to draw up a detailed timetable for accomplishing a fully open EU market and to take action against countries that are delaying the implementation of the directives.

Transmission and Dispatch

According to the directive, Member States are obliged to designate a transmission system operator (TSO), which is responsible for the operation of the high-voltage back-bone, the dispatching of generators, and the establishment of effective interconnections with neighboring transmission grids. The criteria for dispatching must be objective, published and applied in a non-discriminatory manner, so that genuine competition can take place. This implies that the

---

[18] European Commission, DG Competition, "Commission allows merger of VEBA and VIAG subject to stringent conditions" (13 June 2000), IP/00/613 (*www.europa.eu.int*)

[19] Financial Times (29 June 2000)

TSO is not allowed to favor generating facilities belonging to the same company or shareholders of the company in cases where the TSO is not fully separated from production. The criteria must take into account the economic costs of electricity from available generating installations or interconnector transfers, such that those generators with the lowest marginal cost will be dispatched first. This *economic merit order* dispatch will be subject to constraints related to system stability and load profile (i.e. baseload plants, must-run plants, load-following plants, and peaking plants). A Member State may require the TSO to give priority to the dispatching of electricity produced from renewables, waste and from combined heat and power for environmental reasons. This is important as it allows EU governments to encourage the construction of environmentally friendly generation capacity, even in cases where the costs of this electricity exceed the costs of traditionally produced electricity. Eventually, the consumers pay the higher cost as they are rolled over to wholesale and retail tariffs.

Network Access

The directive requires the owners and operators of the electricity networks, i.e. Transmission System Operators and the Distribution System Operators, to provide open access to their infrastructure.[19] The three alternative methods for interconnection, permitted by the directive, are *regulated third party access* (RTPA), *negotiated third party access* (NTPA), and the *single buyer model*. In practice, all Member States have opted for regulated or negotiated third party access— no country will significantly use the single buyer model. Access to transport wires can only be refused when there is insufficient capacity to transport the electricity or when transport would make it impossible to carry out public service obligations.

In the initial phase of liberalization, the single buyer model may be of interest to some MPs with small systems. It should be stressed, however, that the adoption of the single buyer model requires the simultaneous implementation of safeguards to prevent the abuse of market power, as illustrated by the EC provisions. The Internal Market Directive for Electricity stipulates that in "addition to the keeping of separate accounts for the activities of vertically integrated undertakings (unbundling), single buyer activities shall be managed separately from production and distribution activities. No flow of information between the single buyer and the production and distribution companies may take place, except for data that is strictly necessary in order for the single buyer to carry out his responsibilities" (the so-called "Chinese Wall" clause).

Moreover, the EU's version of the single buyer model grants independent producers and autoproducers (those generating power for their own consumption) the right to supply their own premises in the same Member State or in another Member State by using the interconnected system.

Unbundling

In many EU Member States, the national transmission networks are still owned by vertically integrated electricity companies, which generate, transport and sell electricity. Under the new rules, they must permit the use of the transmission network on equal terms to their competitors. If such vertically integrated companies act as TSOs, however, there is a clear risk that they will

---

[19] The networks ("wires") are natural monopolies, while the provision of power via those networks ("services") is potentially competitive, as long as equal access is ensured through effective regulation.

discriminate in favor of their own generation and distribution subsidiaries when granting network access to competitors.

To prevent such discrimination, the directive requires Member States to take three basic measures with regard to vertically integrated power utilities. (i) They are to ensure management unbundling of the TSO. (ii) They must enforce the separation of accounts between electricity generation, transmission, distribution and any other non-electricity activities. For the sake of transparency, these accounts must be published and kept according to standard accounting practices. (iii) And they must ensure that appropriate mechanisms are put in place to prevent confidential information to be passed from the transmission system operator to other parts of the company.

In practice, most Member States have decided to legally separate the TSO from the vertically integrated company, which is the most effective way of ensuring non-discrimination. Spain, the UK (England and Wales), Finland, Sweden, Denmark (west), Austria (east), Ireland, the Netherlands, Portugal, Greece, Italy and some parts of Germany are establishing separate legal entities for the operation of the transmission system, some of them as subsidiaries of the incumbent. Denmark (east), France, UK (Scotland and Northern Ireland), and Austria (west) will ensure that the TSO is independent in management terms.[20] In a precedent-setting case, the Dutch government actually bought the transmission grid from the four vertically integrated companies that owned it, in order to create a fully separate TSO.[21]

Rules for the Construction of New Generation Capacity

In the past, state-owned monopolies had the sole right to build new plants. Now any new capacity they may seek to build, will be subject to scrutiny under EU competition and state-aid laws. Any generation monopolies that continue to exist in some Member States, are thus exposed to potential competition from new entrants. According to the directive, Member States may choose between two different procedures for the construction of new generating capacity: the authorization procedure and the tendering procedure. Whichever procedure a country chooses, it must follow objective, transparent and non-discriminatory criteria.

In the case of the *tendering procedure*, the Government decides on the need for future generating capacity, based on demand estimates carried out by the transmission system operator or any other competent authority designated by the Member State. In the case of the *authorization procedure*, decisions are left to the market and all applications in conformity with generally defined criteria must be authorized.[22] Although the directive provides Member States with a choice between these two approaches for introducing competition (or hybrids thereof), most Member States have opted or will opt for the authorization procedure for the construction of new power plants, as it represents the most transparent and effective mechanism to open up electricity generation to competition.

---

[20] Some countries have more than one transmission grid for geographic or historical reasons.

[21] Financial Times (20 October 2000)

[22] The tendering procedure is similar to the IPP-schemes used by many MPs. In many countries, *merchant plants* are replacing normal IPPs, since they are more compatible with liberalized markets. In the case of an IPP all or most of the risk is taken by parties other than the developer/owner of the plant, through long-term fuel supply agreements, power purchasing agreements etc. In a merchant plant, that risk is borne by the owner.

Public Service Obligations

It is important to note that energy market liberalization and the pursuit of public policies (like social or environmental protection) are fully compatible. In fact, the concept of *public service* plays an important role in the liberalized EU energy market. This approach is clearly reflected in the electricity directive, which permits five categories of public service objectives: (i) environmental considerations, (ii) security, (iii) regularity, (iv) quality of supply constraints and (v) pricing policy considerations. In the pursuit of public policy objectives, however, Member States are obliged to choose policy instruments that minimize market distortions and adverse effects on competition. Moreover, such obligations should be objective, transparent and imposed in a non-discriminatory manner on all operators. Compliance with these strict conditions is being scrutinized by the Commission's DG TREN and DG Competition. Although the directive gives Member States a wide margin of discretion with regard to public service obligations, the policies of individual Member States are converging and fall into three main categories:

- The first category are *universal service obligations* and the overall protection of the consumer, including obligations to connect and supply customers, an obligation to provide power at a standard costs even to remote and rural areas, or special provisions to protect the elderly and disabled.

- The second category is the *protection of the environment*. Some countries oblige transmission companies to purchase environmentally generated electricity at higher prices.

Others impose pollution or fuel taxes to internalize external costs. Most EU Member States support energy saving by consumers through demand side management programs.

- The third category relates to *security of supply*. It comprises technical specifications for all those connected to the grid, reserve capacity requirements, measures to secure the supply of primary fuels for electricity generation, and provisions for the maintenance of a reliable system.

2.3   Regulatory Institutions

The transposition of the EC Internal Market Directives for Electricity and Gas into national law by Member States (discussed in the previous section) has modernized the regulatory framework of energy markets across the EU. To monitor and enforce compliance with this new regulatory framework, however, regulatory agencies are needed. The Commission left it to the individual countries to determine the exact structure and functions of their national regulatory authorities. To ensure a level playing-field across the Single Market, however, the EC monitors developments in the Member States, intervenes when necessary, and has given its full support to the creation of the Council of European Energy Regulators (CEER), described in Box 3 below. As Member States are experimenting with different regulatory models and learning from each other's experience, a convergence towards best practice in regulation should take place.

The majority of EU Member States have created independent energy regulators. In mid-2000, 12 of the 15 EU Member States had independent regulatory authorities for the sector. To balance the interests of consumers and investors and to act in the best interest of the economy at large, regulators need to be sufficiently independent both from the industry they are supposed to regulate (danger of "regulatory capture" by vested interests groups) and from policy makers, which have traditionally interfered in the sector. The task of the regulator is to prevent the abuse of market power and to foster competition. Like in any other industry, this will give energy companies the incentive to cut costs, while ensuring that efficiency gains are being passed on to consumers through lower prices and improved service. At the same time, a transparent and stable regulatory framework should reduce the risk for investors and permit them to earn a reasonable return on their investments. True independence requires not only institutional separation from the utility and the sector ministry, but also access to sufficient resources, adequate staffing policies etc. Documents and websites with further reading on best practice in regulation are listed in the Bibliography.

While most EU countries rely on sector-specific regulation, a few are using cross-sectoral competition policy. As discussed in Box 2, both sector regulation and general competition policy can be used to counter anti-competitive behavior. Competition policy, which relies on a set of general principles, provides a flexible instrument to deal with anti-competitive behavior on a case-to-case basis, but requires a strong competition authority with sophisticated legal and technical expertise. For sectors, where well-defined structural obstacles to competition exist (like natural monopolies in power transmission and distribution), sector-specific regulation permits to address these in a targeted manner (e.g. through unbundling or rules for network access). The main EU country, where the competition authority acts as the energy regulator is Germany. It has a particularly strong and well-respected competition authority, with a specialized department in charge of the energy sector. At the European level, no energy regulator exists but the Commission's Directorate General for Competition (DG Competition)—as the competition authority of the European Union—is also keeping its vigilant eyes on the sector. Since most of the MPs have no or only weak competition policies and anti-trust authorities (with the notable exceptions of Turkey and Israel), however, special energy regulators seems to be the most appropriate tool to drive forward the process of liberalization.

Box 3: The Council of European Energy Regulators (CEER)

An important initiative, which should accelerate the development of effective regulation across the EU, was the establishment of the Council of European Energy Regulators (CEER) in March 2000. A precondition for membership is the full independence of a regulator from its respective government and the CEER currently consists of electricity and gas regulators from 12 EU Member States. In principle, membership and observer status is also open to non-EU energy regulators. The objectives of the CEER are to :

- Establish appropriate regulatory and market mechanisms, in order to achieve competitive European markets in electricity and gas, governed by the principles of transparency and non-discrimination.
- Promote cooperation between regulators and create a forum for the discussion of technical issues and the exchange of experience between them.
- Supply expertise and analysis to policy makers in the energy sector.
- Engage in a dialogue with the institutions of the European Union, representatives of international organizations, and other relevant third parties.
- Develop joint approaches vis-à-vis transnational energy utilities and companies operating in separately regulated utility markets (multi-utilities).
- Where possible, establish common policies and positions between members.

The CEER is expected to become a catalyst for the dissemination of best regulatory practice across EU markets. It could also become an important counterpart for Eastern European and Mediterranean energy regulators, once these countries have established independent regulatory authorities.

2.4 The Development of Electricity Markets and Power Trading

As EU energy companies are adapting to the new policy framework of the sector, specialized energy markets and trading mechanisms are being established. Like any other market, markets for power (and gas) bring together sellers and buyers, match supply with demand, and determine prices. Following the unbundling of vertically integrated utilities, European generation and distribution companies are now trading energy through open and competitive markets.

While long-term power purchasing agreements (PPA) between generators and distributors (or large customers) still make up the lion's share of power sold in the EU, *spot markets* are developing throughout Europe. In national or cross-border *power pools*, an open-bid process ensures that the cheapest power is purchased first. Several power exchanges have already been set up or are in the making. Eventually, competition and consolidation between these exchanges is expected to lead to the emergence of hubs (sub-regions with their own exchanges), within a *multi-hub European Single Market*.

The emergence of a diverse range of trading instruments (e.g. hour-ahead and day-ahead spot prices, future contracts, options) and of specialized intermediaries (e.g. power traders or brokers) are further enhancing the transparency, competitiveness, and efficiency of power markets. All these developments are testimony to private sector dynamics, that tend to unfold once governments provide a conducive legal and regulatory framework. Recent developments in European energy markets include:

- *Standardization of contracts:* Standardized transactions enhance transparency, reduce transaction costs, and increase market liquidity. The European Federation of Energy Traders (EFET, *www.efet.org*), which represent 42 members, has developed a standard contract for the EU single market and encourages large utilities and market participants to adopt it. Nord Pool (see below) is preparing a Financial Energy Master Agreement. The UK has a standard gas trading agreement, and will shortly replace its Electricity Forward Agreement with the Grid Trade Master Agreement.

- *Nord Pool:* In 1996, Norway and Sweden created the world's first cross-border power exchange. Finland joined in 1998 and western Denmark (the country has two grids) in 1999.[24] The exchange is jointly owned on a 50-50 basis by the TSOs of Norway and Sweden. With a combined consumption of 360 TWh/year it is the largest power market in Europe. The Nord Pool spot market determines power flows, while national system operators ensure the physical execution through the exchange of balance power across borders. About 20 percent of all electricity consumed in the region is already being traded on Nord Pool. The creation of the exchange did not require prior privatization, but the transfer of ownership of the interconnectors to independent TSOs in each of the countries. Nord Pool provides a number of trading instruments and services. The *spot market* (Elspot) offers trade in hourly power contracts for physical delivery during the next 24-hour period. Elspot is open to all companies that have signed the necessary agreements and about 200 companies now trade on Nord Pool. The *futures market* (Eltermin) is a purely financial market for price hedging, risk management, and trade in forward and futures power contracts. The trading time horizon is divided into weeks, blocks, seasons and years. About fifteen *brokers* provide services and products to the market. Nord Pool enters into all contracts and reduces counterparty risk through the *clearing of contracts* via the Nordic Power Exchange.[25]

- *UK Power Exchange (UKPX):* The first online trading of electricity contracts started in Britain in June 2000. The UK Power Exchange is owned by OM, operator of the Swedish stock exchange, and is expected to handle a major portion of the £ 6.5 billion annual electricity sales in the UK. In November 2000, the UK will start a new wholesale trading arrangement, replacing the current national pool system. By then, 20-25 percent of all electricity sales are expected to be conducted through screen-based trading. Generators and customers will be free to trade electricity through online markets up to 3.5 hours before physical delivery. UKPX is already offering forward contracts up to 1.5 years.

---

[24] In May 2000, Nord Pool threatened to exclude Denmark, unless the Jylland monopolist Elsam opened its network to foreign competitors (due to the small size of the market, the only competition can come from abroad). NERA, Global Energy Regulation Newsletter (May 2000)

[25] Information on Nord Pool from Financial Times (18 January 2000) and World Bank Viewpoint No. 162, "International Power Trade – The Nordic Power Pool" (January 1999)

Box 4 a) The European Association of Transmission System Operators (ETSO)

Across Europe, physical interconnections between national grid systems have long been in place. If the EU single market for power is to become a reality, however, complementary institutional and regulatory structures have to be established. Generating companies can only sell electricity to their customers (distribution companies or large users), if they have access to the transmission network. Cross-border power trade and the creation of trans-national power markets are simplified considerably, if the transmission companies of different countries cooperate on issues like cross-border pricing, or congestion management. To facilitate the cross-border integration of European transmission networks, the European Association of Transmission System Operators (ETSO) was established in July 1999. ETSO is an example of the principle of subsidiarity, whereby the Commission provides an EU-wide regulatory framework for the sector but leaves the fine-tuning of market structures to national governments, regulators, and industry participants.

In March 2000, ETSO members and other concerned parties (e.g. regulators, power traders, officials from the EC and EU countries) met in Florence to take an important step towards the creation of a competitive pan-European power market. The *Florence Process* ties up some loose ends of the electricity directive. ETSO proposed pricing and settlement mechanisms for cross-border trades, which were to come into effect in October 2000. After a period of one year, the regime will be evaluated and fine-tuned. ETSO is also in the process of establishing a network to exchange systems management data between national TSOs, the first component of which should come on stream at the end of 2000. Moreover, ETSO has started to work on the issue of congestion management and has given a first recommendation on a contentious case (it proposed to *auction* scarce network capacity). It also acts as a forum for the exchange of experience between national TSOs (e.g. a benchmarking task force has been established), as well as a consultation body that interacts with policy makers and other market participants on behalf of its members.

ETSO members include the TSOs from the 15 EU countries, as well as those from Norway and Switzerland. Applications from EU accession countries will be considered, once these have implemented the provisions of the electricity directive. ETSO has a rotating presidency and secretariat and has established a website (*www.etso-net.org*). While it is a young institution and still in the process of developing its structures and work practices, it could eventually become an important partner in the establishment of the Mediterranean Energy Ring and the creation of cross-border power markets in the southern Mediterranean.

Box 4 b) The Union for the Coordination of the Transmission of Electricity (UCTE)

Whereas ETSO is primarily concerned with the economic aspects of interconnection and was founded to help implement the EU electricity directive, UCTE's mandate is to secure the technical integrity and stability of the continental European grid. In fact, UCTE (*www.ucte.org*) was a founding member of ETSO and both organizations, whose memberships overlap, cooperate closely. UCTE sets technical standards and rules for system management. Two dispatching centers in Germany and Switzerland coordinate the operation of the synchronized interconnected system. Founded 50 years ago, UCTE has 16 members (the EU countries on the European mainland, Switzerland, and the countries of former Yugoslavia) as well as four associated members (Poland, the Slovak Republic, the Czech Republic, and Hungary). Bulgaria and Romania are currently adapting their systems to UCTE standards. The closing of the Mediterranean Electricity Ring (see Chapter 4) would have important technical implications for the system of continental Europe if the two were to be synchronized. Hence, UCTE maintains a dialogue with its Mediterranean equivalents *Medelec* (Mediterranean Liaison Committee of Associations of Electricity Supply Undertakings), of which it is also a member, and *COMELEC* (for the Maghreb).

- *Amsterdam Power Exchange (APX):* Like most exchanges, the Amsterdam Power Exchange is owned by the market participants. APX started operation in May 1999 as a day-ahead spot market with prices published daily for greater transparency and benchmarking purposes. The fully electronic power exchange is currently in the process of developing advanced trading products. Examples are a Bulletin Board for bilateral trading, the Hour-Ahead Market and the Futures and Forwards market for long-term contracts. APX has the ambition to become a regional hub for physical and financial power trading and launched trading on its German Hub in May 2000. This will put it into direct competition with the *Leipzig Power Exchange* (using the trading system of Nord Pool) and the *Frankfurt Power Exchange*, which both began operation in mid-2000. Market participants and authorities interested in setting up similar power trading systems in their own countries can participate in a special training and simulation program on the different trading products used by APX.

- *Automated Power Exchange (US and UK):* The Automated Power Exchange Inc. offers internet-based trading in some U.S. States and plans to start operating in England and Wales in the summer of 2000, prior to the start of the New Electricity Trading Arrangements. US participants on APX exchanges trade mainly for physical delivery, but APX systems can also be used for financial trading. APX's UK operation will be open to all generators, supply companies, traders and large end-users.

- *European Energy Exchange (EEX):* The European Energy Exchange was founded in November 1999, with the initial objective of facilitating power trading between Germany and Switzerland. It was scheduled to start next-day spot trading and dealings in futures before the end of 2000. At a latter date, EEX plans to expand to trading in oil, gas, weather derivatives and emissions certificates. EEX is 48 percent owned by Eurex, the European derivatives exchange, and 52 percent by financial institutions, utilities and large industrial consumers.

2.5 <u>Restructuring at the Utility Level</u>

The legal and regulatory reforms at the policy level are exerting significant pressure on European utilities to cut costs, restructure, and become more competitive. Unlike in many of the MPs, European power and gas utilities have long been commercialized and corporatized. Now, liberalization, unbundling, privatization, and cross-border integration are creating a whole new set of challenges. Restructuring at the utility-level has considerably increased the efficiency and rate of innovation in the entire sector; it has reduced costs to customers and taxpayers; and it is creating competitive companies that should prosper in global markets. The speed at which changes were introduced made the transition at times painful. But those companies that were ready to adjust quickly, have been able to exploit new market opportunities and expand across borders.

The unbundling of vertically integrated companies into generation, transmission, and distribution as required by the directive, implies not only a separation of accounts and the division of assets between the resulting units. In those countries that opted for full unbundling, it also requires the establishment of new legal and organizational entities. Unbundled companies or subsidiaries have to learn to interact through open power markets, instead of the internal structures of a vertically integrated company. Transmission System Operators (TSOs) have to acquire the technical, financial, and legal skills needed to manage a system with open access and merit-order dispatch. Generators and distributors have to become familiar with the design and negotiation of contracts, the clearing of trades, or the use of market intermediaries. In Member States where former state monopolies have not only been unbundled vertically but also horizontally (i.e. disposal of generation capacity or geographical division of the distribution network), additional restructuring is required (see Section 2.1).

The full separation of operational and regulatory functions poses another set of restructuring challenges. Former state-monopolies, used to a cozy relationship with policy makers, are now accountable to market mechanisms and independent regulators. They can no longer rely on political protection or monopoly rents. They have to keep accounts in compliance with general accounting standards and are obliged to share commercial information with energy regulators. Strict EU state aid rules, enforced by the Commission's DG for Competition, mean that operational or investment subsidies are no longer permitted. Privatization further severs the links between utilities and politicians. The management of privatized companies are fully exposed to the disciplines of capital markets, which demand efficiency and a reasonable return to investment. However, privatization has also empowered them by providing the opportunity to tap capital markets to finance investments and expand into new markets.

Perhaps the biggest incentive for restructuring has come from increased national and cross-border competition. Pressure on prices has eroded inflated margins and forced utilities to bring tariffs in line with actual costs. More importantly, it has created pressure to dramatically increase efficiency by laying off surplus staff, streamlining organizational structures, adopting modern management techniques, and acquiring more efficient technology. As competition has given customers the freedom to shop around, former monopolies can no longer rely on a captive client base. Instead, they have to sharpen their marketing skills, become service oriented and responsive to customer needs, and introduce state-of-the-art information technology for billing and client management. An interesting example for latter is a project which the association of German energy generators announced in August 2000. Its 900 members are to harmonize the way they collect and process customer information. From 2001, data can be exchanged through a central computer to facilitate the transfer of clients between competitors.[26]

Another facet of restructuring at the utility-level is the rapid consolidation of power companies though mergers and acquisitions. With a transaction volume of more than $ 20 billion in 1999, Europe was the most important energy M&A market world-wide. Deals involving European utilities included the purchase of London Electricity by Suez-Lyonnaise for $ 3.2 billion; IVO's acquisition of Stockholm Energi for $ 2 billion; the completion of EdF's take-over of Tractebel (Belgium) for $ 7.9 billion; Endesa's (Spain) acquisition of 64 percent in Endesa Chile for $ 2.1 billion; or PowerGen's (UK) purchase of Louisville Gas and Electric (US) for $ 5.4 billion. A good indicator for how far the process of cross-border consolidation has advanced, is the fact that virtually all of Belgium's and 75 percent of Dutch generation is now foreign-owned. Domestic and cross-border M&As are expected to remain a prominent feature in EU power markets for the foreseeable future. Many observers predict the emergence of a handful of pan-European utilities over the coming decade, which should become strong players on the global stage.

---

[26] Süddeutsche Zeitung (22 August 2000)

Box 5: The Union of the Electricity Industry (EURELECTRIC)

The Union of the Electricity Industry (EURELECTRIC) is the umbrella organization of national electricity associations and electricity companies in the EU and neighboring regions. Based in Brussels, it has been formed through the 1999 merger between UNIPEDE (the international union of electricity producers and distributors) and EURELECTRIC (set up to represent the interests of the electricity industry vis-à-vis the EU institutions). It used to have national incumbents as individual members, but in the future only national associations, open to all electricity companies (generators, transmission companies, distributors, electricity traders), will be eligible for membership. Full members include all 15 EU countries, the other OECD countries in Europe and (since recently) all EU accession countries (except for Bulgaria). To take account of industry unbundling in the EU, EURELECTRIC has created four Business Areas: generation, transmission, distribution, and supply. The main topics it deals with are energy policy and market structure; environment and sustainability; and management practices for the electricity industry.

One of the key objectives of EURELECTRIC is to help European electricity companies to adapt to the changing market environment. The organization provides a wide range of services and information on the energy sector through (i) its trimestrial industry newsletter *Watt's New*; (ii) technical publications (e.g. on unbundling); (iii) conferences, working groups, study tours; (iv) and through its revamped website (*www.eurelectric.org*). The latter contains industry reports and studies, position papers, press releases, information about upcoming events, as well as conference proceedings and information about its members. EURELECTRIC's *industry observatory* helps to harmonize, gather, and disseminate energy statistics through an annual publication and increasingly through the Internet. Moreover, it recently established a Network of Experts on Benchmarking to develop a more coherent approach to this important issue.

EURELECTRIC is also gearing up to help utilities in EU accession countries and those of the southern Mediterranean rim in the process of restructuring. Most of the accession countries have recently become full members and receive assistance through research, conferences, study tours, twinning arrangements, and small-scale technical assistance. EURELECTRIC is also contributing to the joint World Bank-European Commission Action Plan for energy reforms in the accession countries (see text-box in Chapter 4). In early 2000, a new *Mediterranean Desk* was created, to assist affiliate members in the Middle East and North Africa region (a new membership category). So far, EURELECTRIC's Mediterranean members are Morocco, Algeria, Tunisia, Egypt, and Israel. EURELECTRIC is expected to become a key counterpart for the regional Meda energy project for Energy Company Restructuring (for details see Chapter 4).

According to EURELECTRIC's *Annual Report* 1999, the "world-wide electricity markets are caught up in an irreversible trend towards deregulation, liberalization and privatization. At the European level, the application by law, since February 1999, of the Internal Market Directive, has led to the most complex restructuring the sector has ever experienced. [...] This existing business environment [is] radically re-shaping the traditional face of the Industry and rapidly transforming it into a dynamic and innovative service sector. [EURELECTRIC] is fully committed to actively [...] maintaining its position at the forefront of the Electricity Industry."

2.6   Cross-Border Electricity Markets and EU Enlargement

One of the most intriguing aspects of EU electricity reforms is the cross-border integration of power markets across the continent. It could provide some interesting lessons for greater integration in the Mediterranean region. At present, 8 percent of total power generated in the EU is being traded between countries. National grids have long been interconnected and trade of electricity among EU countries has been widespread for many years (see Box 5 above). However, these transactions have mainly taken place under bilateral contracts and not within the context of a competitive market. A number of developments outlined in the sections above are now driving market integration across the EU. The Internal Market Directives for Electricity and Gas as well as EU competition and state aid law provide for a level playing field across all 15 Member States. Cooperation of national regulators through the Council of European Energy Regulators (CEER) will lead to further harmonization of the regulatory framework. Open network access, the unbundling of transmission, cross-border cooperation between TSOs, as well as the emergence of regional power exchanges, will permit buyers and sellers to trade freely across borders. Finally, trans-national mergers and acquisitions between energy companies will complete the Single Market at the utility-level.

The EU Single Market for energy is not only becoming deeper but also broader. Ten Central and Eastern European (CEE) countries, as well as the three Euro-Mediterranean Partners (MPs) Turkey, Cyprus, and Malta are official EU accession candidates.[27] One of the main conditions for membership is the adoption of EU legislation (*acquis communautaire*), including the electricity and gas directives. Over the coming decade, the candidate countries are thus expected to fully liberalize and largely privatize their energy markets, and to integrate them closely with those of the EU. The developments in Central and Eastern Europe are of relevance to the Maghreb and Mashrek countries for a number of reasons. First, the MPs can learn from the reform experience of their CEE peers. Second, they will have to match the economic performance of the CEE countries, if they want to compete successfully for exports to the EU market as well as foreign investment. Third, by the time the FTA is completed by around 2010, most accession candidates are likely to be part of the EU and the EU's Single Market for energy is likely to comprise up to 30 countries. It is expected to be fully liberalized, privatized, and integrated. EU energy companies will be lean and competitive. Finally, three of the MPs (Turkey, Cyprus, and Malta) are actually part of the accession process. To illustrate current developments in the CEE, the electricity sector policies of two leading reformers (Poland and Hungary) are briefly outlined below.

Poland

Both in terms of population (40 million) and market size (GNP: $ 140 billion), Poland is the largest accession candidate in Central and Eastern Europe. The reform of the Polish power sector started in 1997. A new energy law established the Energy Regulatory Authority and set out the principles for third-party access.[28] In the early 1990s, the industry was unbundled and a TSO was established (the Polish Power Grid, PSE). The generation sector was divided in 17 power plants and 19 combined heat-and-power plants and the distribution sector into 33 regional companies. Over the past five years, Poland has also re-balanced its tariff structure to reduce the degree of cross-subsidization and ensure full cost-recovery. Its ratio of average residential tariffs to average industrial tariffs (one of the most commonly used indicators for distortions in the price

---

[27] The ten CEE accession candidates are Poland, the Czech Republic, Slovak Republic, Hungary, Slovenia, Bulgaria, Romania, Estonia, Lithuania, and Latvia.

[28] "Electricity in Poland: Living by the Market Rules", W. Mielczarski, Power Economics (April 2000).

structure), is 1.8. This is the highest in the region (Hungary has 1.4 and the Czech Republic 1.1) and is close to the 2.0 average of European OECD countries.

After the modernization of the legal framework, sector unbundling, and tariff reform, the government has started to introduce competition. Domestic market opening began in August 1998 for customers with over 100 GWh of annual consumption (representing 34 percent of the total market) and reached customers with demand over 40 GWh in January 2000 (43 percent). By December 2005, 100 percent of Poland's power market is supposed to be opened to competition. In 2002, restrictions on electricity imports will be lifted and third-party access should be extended to imports from EU countries.

With the new legal and regulatory framework in place, the Government has launched a privatization program. In May 1998, EdF acquired 55 percent of Krakow CHP. The Bedzin and Wroclaw CHPs were floated on the Warsaw stock exchange. At the end of 1999, a 38 percent stake in the generation group Patnow-Adamow-Konin was sold for $ 188 million to Elektrim. In January 2000, Vattenfall bought 55 percent of Warsaw CHP for $ 235 million. In April 2000, Tractebel (owned by Suez Lyonnaise des Eaux) purchased a 25 percent stake in Poland's fifth-largest generator for $ 84 million. Two months later, EdF and GdF acquired 45 percent in the Wybrzeze CHP for $ 62 million. Germany's RWE and two Japanese firms are lining up to bid for Poland's largest power plant, Belchatów. In mid-2000, several companies were preparing to bid for GZE, the country's largest distribution company. The first IPP in Poland, a 120 MW plant in Nowa Sarzyna owned by Enron, recently came on stream. In total, 10 generation plants and one distribution company are currently in various stages of privatization. The target is to first find strategic investors for a significant share in each company and then sell the remainder to financial investors.

In July 2000 trading on the new *Polish Power Exchange (PPE)*, the first one in Central and Eastern Europe, started.[29] The main owners are the Treasury (30 percent), the Polish conglomerate Elektrim, the Spanish utility Endesa, the Warsaw stock exchange, and the Polish power grid (10 percent each). It started with day-ahead spot transactions and will be extended to hour-ahead and derivatives trading a year later. Participants in the exchange hope that it will evolve into a regional trading hub for Eastern Europe, including the Czech Republic, Slovakia, and the Baltic states.[30] In a separate development but as part of broader energy sector reforms, the government decided in June 2000 to split the public oil and gas company into an infrastructure unit, four distribution companies, and an exploration and production company, prior to their privatization in 2001.[31]

Hungary

Hungary began to re-structure its power sector in 1992. The state-owned monopoly MVM was unbundled and only retained ownership of the high-voltage grid and dispatch center, with the mandate to manage all trade in electricity. Eight generation companies (gencos), six regional distribution companies (discos), and a network maintenance company were spun off. In 1994 the Electricity Act was passed and the Hungarian Energy Office, an energy regulator with only

---

[29] During the first month of operation, 28 participants already traded one percent of the country's electricity, according to Power in Eastern Europe (11 August 2000).

[30] Financial Times (13 June 2000)

[31] East European Energy Report (26 June 2000)

limited independence, was set up. The government opted for a single-buyer model with long-term power purchasing agreements between MVM and generation companies. This will reduce the ability of the government to introduce more competitive market mechanisms and to gradually liberalize the sector, in compliance with the EU energy *acquis*.[32] As the first step in that direction, the government decided to open the market for large users (about 10 percent of the market) from July 2001.[33] Electricity prices are still low (for households 45 percent of the EU average) but a new tariff regime, introduced in 1999, prohibits cross-subsidies between different groups of customers. A small consumer protection system is meant to minimize the social impact of tariff-rebalancing.

Since most of the thermal capacity was old, there is a need for large-scale new investments. Hungary became the first country in Central and Eastern Europe to offer domestic and foreign investors majority control in generation and distribution companies. All non-nuclear generating assets were transferred to the State Privatization and Holding Co., which then sold these assets. In 1995 and 1996 five of eight generation companies and all six distribution companies were sold for a total of $ 1.5 billion. Foreign strategic investors now hold majority stakes in most of the generation and distribution companies. On balance, Hungary has made more progress in privatization than in liberalization.

---

[32] Power Economics (July 1999)
[33] NERA Global Energy Regulation (June 2000)

Chapter 3

Power Sector Policies of the Mediterranean Partners

3   POWER SECTOR POLICIES OF THE MEDITERRANEAN PARTNERS

3.1   Introduction

Energy sector reform in the southern Mediterranean region—and particularly in the Maghreb and Mashrek countries—is still in its infant stage and far behind Europe and other emerging market economies. The market structure and policy framework in most of the MPs continues to be dominated by vertically integrated, state-owned monopolies. Regulatory and operational functions tend to be insufficiently separated and many utilities have not yet been corporatized. Few countries in the region have a transparent regulatory framework and none of the Maghreb and Mashrek countries has an independent regulator. Legal frameworks are often outdated and sector institutions weak. Direct and indirect subsidies are widespread, as are price distortions.

With GDP growth rates that are low by international standards, electricity demand growth across the MPs has been a disproportionately high. At 7.4 percent between 1990 and 1998 it was the highest in the world, compared to a global average of 2.3 percent.[33] Much of this is due to low sector efficiency (e.g. system losses) and price subsidies. Projected increases in energy demand will require significant investment over the coming decade, putting further strains on government budgets unless private capital can be mobilized. According to most estimates a total of 20,000 to 30,000 MW of new capacity will have to be installed in the 12 MPs over the coming decade, if demand continues to grow at current rates.

Table 1:   Selected Power Sector Indicators by Country (1998)

Country	Population	GDP	Installed Capacity	Power Generation	Demand Growth (1990–98)	System Losses
	(million)	(billion $)	(MW)	(GWh, net)	(% p.a.)	(%)
Algeria	30	47	5,536	21,971	4.5	25
Cyprus	0.8	9	728	2,811	4.7	n.a.
Egypt	61	83	14,503	60,888	5.6	17
Israel	6	101	9,500	34,831	7.5	n.a.
Jordan	5	7	1,670	6,345	8.3	16
Lebanon	4	17	2,139	8,357	24.0	44
Malta	0.4	4	572	1,612	5.2	n.a.
Morocco	28	36	3,675	12,483	5.5	18
Syria	15	17	4,430	11,755	5.8	25
Tunisia	9	20	1,719	8,672	5.6	12
Turkey	63	199	21,889	105,499	9.2	20
WB&G*	3	3	n.a.	n.a.	n.a.	n.a.
Total / Av.	**225**	**543**	**66,010**	**275,214**	**7.4**	**22**

*West Bank and Gaza
Source: World Bank / IEA / EIA / UN / *Financial Times.*

Reliable and consistent data for the countries of the region is scarce (on this problem see also Section 4.2). Anecdotal evidence and the few efficiency indicators available (e.g. system losses or

---

[33] "The Euromediterranean Energy Partnership" by Debra Johnson, Financial Times Energy (June 2000)

government subsidies), however, illustrate the need for policy reform and utility restructuring. An international survey on competition and regulation in the energy sector, published by the World Bank in 1999, shows that North Africa and the Middle East lags considerably behind other developing regions.[35] The study covered 115 countries, including seven of the Mediterranean Partners, and was the most comprehensive analysis carried out with regard to energy sector reform in the developing world. Reform indicators used were: the existence of an independent regulator; private participation in generation and distribution; the commercialization and corporatization of the state utility; and the enactment of a sector law that permits unbundling and privatization. Table 2 provides detailed information about reform measures undertaken by individual MPs (1 = reform implemented, 0 = reform not implemented) and shows that sector restructuring in the region still has a long way to go.

Table 2:   Status of Power Sector Reform in the 12 Mediterranean Partners

Country	Commercialized/ Corporatized	Law	Independent Regulator	IPPs	Utility Restructured	Generation Private	Distribution Private	Reform Indicator
Algeria	0	0	0	0	0	0	0	0
Cyprus*	n.a.	n.a.	n.a.	n.a.	n.a.	n.a.	n.a.	n.a.
Egypt	0	0	0	1**	0	0	0	1
Israel*	1	0	1	1	0	0	0	3
Jordan	1	1	0	0	1	0	1**	4
Lebanon	0	0	0	0	0	0	0	0
Malta*	n.a.	n.a.	n.a.	n.a.	n.a.	n.a.	n.a.	n.a.
Morocco	0	0	0	1	0	1	1	3
Pales. Auth.*	0	0	0	0	0	0	0	0
Syria*	0	0	0	0	0	0	0	0
Tunisia	0	0	0	1**	0	0	0	1
Turkey	1	1	0	1	0	1	0	4

** not shown in Bacon Study. 1 = reform implemented ; 0 = reform not implemented. Note: Countries marked with a * were not included in the World Bank Bacon Study and the information shown in the table is drawn from other sources.
Source: World Bank.

By adding the figures for individual policies, a rough reform score can be calculated for each country. Averaging country scores yields reform indices for world regions. Table 3 shows the reform scores for the power sector in different developing regions, which the Bacon study generated. The Middle East and North Africa (MENA) ranks last, after Sub-Saharan Africa (SSA).[36] The large difference in bar size illustrates how much more reforms have advanced in Latin American and the Caribbean (LAC); South Asia (SA); Eastern Europe and Central Asia (ECA); and East Asia and the Pacific region (EAP).

---

[35] "A Scorecard for Energy Reform in the Developing Countries", World Bank Viewpoint No. 175 (April 1999). This survey covers the electricity, oil and gas sectors.

[36] It should be noted that the geographical definition of the region, used in this study, includes the countries of the Arab Peninsula, but not Israel, Turkey, Cyprus, and Malta.

Diagram 6: Power Sector Reform Indicators By World Region

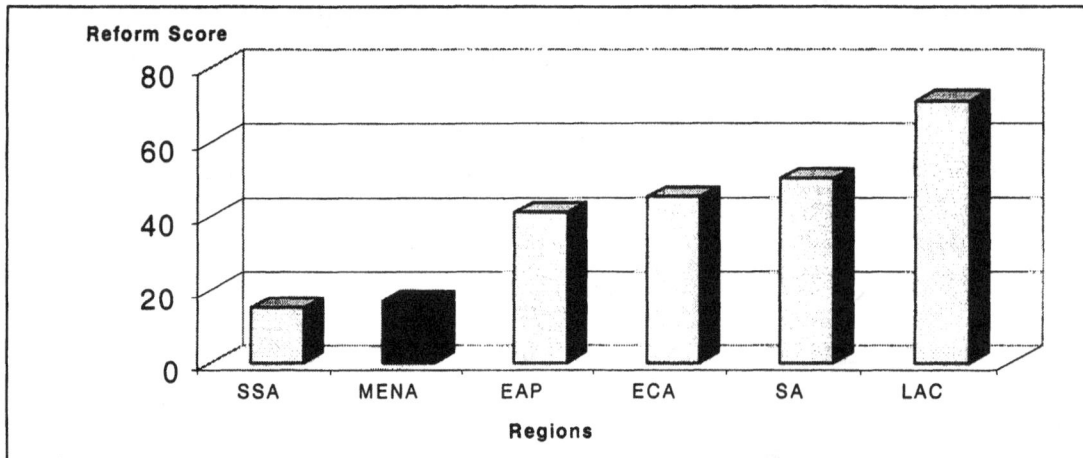

Reform Score

Regions

Source: World Bank.

Despite this general pattern, several of the MPs have initiated reforms. In Jordan, a significant part of the distribution sector has traditionally been privately owned. A new sector law from July 1999 provides for the establishment of an energy regulator and the unbundling of the National Electric Power Company (NEPCO); a privatization strategy for the subsidiaries was to be drawn up by September 2001. In Egypt, a February 1998 sector law created 7 regional generation and distribution companies. Partial privatization of these companies was planned but then delayed indefinitely. The country has successfully mobilized private investment for the construction of a domestic transmission and distribution network for natural gas. In many countries, including Egypt, Morocco, Tunisia, Turkey, Israel, and Jordan, independent power plants (IPPs) are being introduced through international competitive tenders. After years of hesitation, Turkey finally began with what could become the most ambitious liberalization and privatization strategy in the region.

While these and other reforms are important first steps, the MPs still face significant reform challenges. Many of them have yet to begin to overhaul the legal, regulatory and institutional framework of their energy sector and to restructure their energy companies. In others, reform have thus far been lopsided (e.g. private participation without adequate competition or regulation), piecemeal (e.g. minority privatizations with no impact on corporate governance), sub-optimally sequenced (e.g. IPPs prior to regulatory reform), or inconsistent with international best practice (e.g. the vertical integration of formerly independent generation and distribution companies in Egypt). Diagram 7 shows that the Middle East and North Africa region has attracted considerably less private investment in the energy sector than other developing regions such as Latin America.[36] More interestingly, the break-down shows that greenfield projects and more limited forms of private participation (like operation and maintenance projects) dominate. The actual privatization of state assets in the energy sector, usually an indicator for more far-reaching reforms, does not feature at all. This contrasts sharply with the situation in Latin America.

---

[36] It should be noted that the regional definition for the Middle East and North Africa, which is used here (and follows the general World Bank definition) does not include Turkey, Israel, Cyprus, and Malta, but some of the Gulf countries. When comparing the figures between regions, one should also keep in mind that they differ in terms of population and the size of their economies.

Diagram 7: Private Investment in Energy Projects by Region and Type (1990–99)

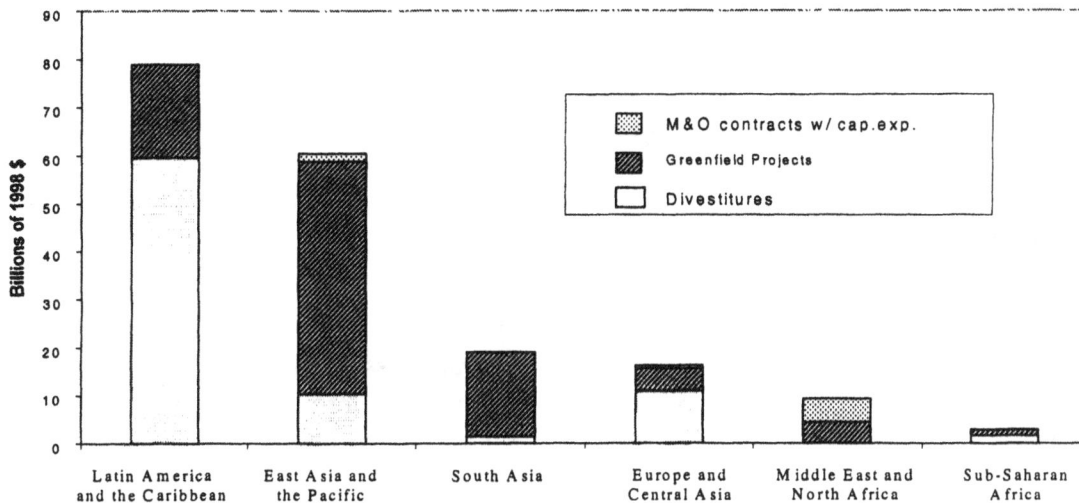

Source: World Bank.

3.2   Policy Challenges and Reform Efforts in Individual MPs

TURKEY: *After years of delay and initial mistakes with IPPs, comprehensive reforms have been launched in preparation for EU accession.*

- Turkey started with the implementation of a comprehensive reform strategy in 1999, following a decade of stop-and-go reforms and abortive attempts to address the structural problems of its energy sector (an intransparent institutional and legal framework, enormous investment needs, system losses of 20 percent, fast growing power demand etc.).[37] It is a cornerstone of a broader adjustment program supported by the World Bank and the IMF.

- One specific difficulty Turkey has to address is the legacy of IPPs which were introduced into an unreformed sector. Since the 1980s, four BOTs with a total installed capacity of 1,810 MW and combined project costs of $ 2.5 billion have been constructed. By 1999, 13 percent of generation capacity was private.[38] Facing a non-transparent and unpredictable regulatory framework, however, investors demanded comprehensive government guarantees to build BOT power plants. The treasury assumed price risk, market risk, and indirectly fuel supply risk, which left the government (and thus taxpayers) with significant contingent liabilities. Teas, the state-owned utility, now buys IPP power at 8 to 9 c/kWh, but re-sells it at a mere

---

[37] According to Euromoney (February 2000), "In terms of forecast investment, Turkey is the fourth-largest electricity market in the world [...] the government plans to add 40,000 MW of capacity by 2010. [...] The Turkish Electricity Generation Transmission Company (Teas) claims that Turkey needs to spend more than $ 5.5 billion a year on power and that investment required by the end of 2020 is $ 127.8 billion. [...] But [...] things are moving at a glacial speed because the political, economic and legal environment is not up to the requirements of the situation. [...] There is no central energy authority and energy planning is far from seamless. A dozen public-sector and private-sector agencies, each reporting to different authorities, are involved. There is a wide range of laws and regulations matched in scope by loopholes and pitfalls."

[38] Euromoney (February 2000).

6.8 c/kWh, incurring substantial losses in the process.[39] Moreover, the existence of long-term commitments from the concession contracts is now limiting the scope for sector reforms.

- The main feature of the sector strategy the government adopted under the ongoing WB-sponsored National Transmission Grid Project and a proposed Economic Reform Project, is the withdrawal of the state from ownership and operations. Transmission is to be unbundled from generation and distribution, with the government-owned systems operator ensuring open network access. The state plans to privatize its remaining generation and distribution assets. An independent regulatory commission is to be set up to ensure fair competition and protect consumer interests.

- A directive has already been issued, which provides for the division of the state-owned generation and transmission company TEAS into a transmission company, a generation company (to be privatized), and a trading company (to take over long term power purchasing agreements with private IPPs). An Electricity Market Law, under preparation with TA from the World Bank, will pave the way for the creation of the regulatory commission and remove legal restrictions on the sale of electricity assets.

- Another important reform, which required the amendment of the constitution, was the enactment of a law permitting international arbitration in the settling of business disputes in January 2000. By giving reassurance to foreign investors, who were reluctant to rely on Turkish courts, it will reduce the risk premium they demand for investments in the country. The Energy Minister has estimated that this could unlock planned infrastructure projects worth up to $ 22 billion, including several large build-operate-transfer (BOT) power plants.[40]

- Liberalization, restructuring, and privatization are also under way in the gas and petroleum sector. Amendments to an existing law are currently being drafted, in order to split the vertically integrated state-monopoly BOTAS into three separate companies for transmission, trading, and distribution. The transmission company (to remain publicly owned) is to concentrate on the expansion of the national gas network and will have a mandate to ensure open access. Distribution is to be sub-divided along geographical lines prior to privatization. In early 2000, the state refining company TUPRAS and the gasoline marketing company POAS (with an extensive network of petrol stations) were partially privatized for more than $ 2.5 billion.[41]

- Turkey was recently recognized as a candidate country for EU accession and both the Turkish government and the World Bank, which is providing significant technical assistance in support of sector restructuring, are making an effort to ensure compatibility of reforms with the EU's *acquis communautaire* in the energy sector. As a first step towards closer integration with EU energy markets, Turkey and Greece recently agreed to go ahead with a $ 500 million, 400-600 MW IPP, which is to be built in Greece but supply the Turkish market.[42] At the same time, the two countries intend to build a high-voltage interconnector, linking Turkey to the EU-UCTE grid.

---

[39] Financial Times (12 June 2000)

[40] MEED (4 February 2000)

[41] 51 percent of POAS was sold for $ 1,260 million and 31.5 percent of TUPRAS for $ 1,300 million.

[42] In January 2000, an international consortium launched the feasibility study for the project, which would be the first private power plant in Greece. MEED (28 January 2000)

Box 6: The Drawbacks of Independent Power Plants (IPPs)

Independent Power Plants (IPPs) have a number of advantages. First, they permit the introduction of private investment in a government-dominated sector and can help a country to attract FDI, provided these investments come from abroad. Second, private management and a commercial incentive to minimize costs, often considerably increase the operational efficiency in generation. Third, a well managed and transparent tender process with international competitive bidding, can ensure that savings are passed on to consumers and taxpayers. Egypt is a case in point. The IPP in Sidi Krir will mobilize about $ 400 million of private investments; the plant is expected to be run with only one fifth of the staff of comparable publicly-owned power stations; and the IPP will sell power for a mere 2.6 c/kWh to the network.

Unfortunately, as many countries in Asia and elsewhere have painfully discovered, IPPs are a sub-optimal approach to sector reform and have considerable drawbacks. First, the main economic benefits of sector reforms are derived from liberalization, but IPPs are no effective instrument to introduce competition. On the contrary, the long-run power-purchasing agreements (PPAs) associated with IPPs preclude real competition between generators. Second, IPPs only introduce private participation in the generation sub-sector and even here they merely affect new (greenfield) projects, but not the much larger stock of existing plants (unless an IPP scheme includes the transfer and rehabilitation of existing facilities). Third, the introduction of private participation through IPPs prior to comprehensive sector reform, creates property rights and political commitments. These lead to policy lock-in and considerably reduce the scope for future reforms. Finally, long-term PPAs and fuel purchasing agreements (lasting a decade and more) can lead to stranded assets or to large liabilities for state-owned transmission and distribution companies. The public Turkish utility Teas, for example, has to pay 8 to 9 c/kWh for power from IPPs, which it resells at a loss for 6.8 c/kWh. In many MPs, investors are practically shielded from risk (e.g. demand risk, currency risk), leaving governments with contingent liabilities that often amount to billions of dollars.

The heyday of the IPP was the period between 1992 and 1996. The region which most enthusiastically endorsed this approach was Asia, accounting for more than three quarters of global IPP investments. But the 1997 financial crisis abruptly ended this honeymoon. State-owned transmission and distribution companies (as the off-takers for IPP-generated power) had signed PPAs, denominated in foreign currency, while their revenues were in domestic currency. When the currencies of their countries depreciated dramatically and when previous estimates of power demand turned out to be overly optimistic, they were forced to purchase electricity they did not need at prices they could no longer afford. This painful experience and the good performance of countries that opted for liberalization (e.g. in Latin America) convinced Asian countries to embrace more comprehensive sector reform. Korea has committed itself to introduce a competitive power pool by 2003. In Thailand, the state utility is to be unbundled and privatized and a wholesale electricity market is to be established by 2003. Indonesia plans to unbundle the sector and gradually create a fully competitive power market. The Philippines and China have also launched broad sector reforms.

In the southern Mediterranean, Turkey and Morocco have pioneered the use of IPPs, as discussed in the respective country sections. Like countries in Asia, Turkey is also moving away from this piecemeal approach to sector restructuring. In Morocco, the large IPP of Jorf Lasfar has attracted significant investments but will make future liberalization much more difficult, especially since it represents a large share of the total market. Other countries in the region are now considering the introduction of IPPs. They would be well advised to take a close look at the Asian experience on the one hand and at the lessons from regions that embraced more comprehensive sector reform, like the EU and Latin America. In those cases where they opt for IPPs, nonetheless, they should only do so after developing a coherent long-term strategy for the sector, like Jordan has done.

Note: For further information on IPPs, please refer to the Bibliography.

CYPRUS & MALTA: *The two island economies with small energy markets are preparing for EU accession.*

- Cyprus and Malta have started EU accession negotiations and will have to transpose the Internal Directives for Electricity and Gas, as well as other pieces of EU energy legislation.

- The small size of their electricity and gas sectors (small systems) combined with the fact that they are islands without interconnections to the international grid, will make special arrangements necessary. These countries will probably apply for derogations from the unbundling requirements, similar to those given to Luxembourg.

- The government of Cyprus has declared its intention to comply with the energy *acquis* by 2003 and at the time of writing (mid-2000), consultants had been hired to assist in the development of a reform strategy for the sector.

- In Malta, the state monopoly for electricity and petroleum (Enemalta) is to be unbundled into financially independent generation, transmission, and distribution units, while non-electric activities are to be spun off. Cross-subsidization will no longer be permitted and an independent regulator will take over the regulatory functions (e.g. the issuing of licenses) currently carried out by Enemalta.

JORDAN: *Reforms are well-designed and carefully sequenced, but yet to be fully implemented.*

- Throughout the Mashrek and Maghreb, Jordan is arguably the most advanced country with regard to energy sector reforms. Distribution has largely been privately owned for several decades. The Jordanian Electric Power Company Ltd. (Jepco) and the Irbid District Electric Power Company (Ideco) have concessions dating back to 1938 and 1957 and presently control about 60 percent of the total distribution market. They have long struggled with the uncertainties and non-transparency of the regulatory framework

- The government started to unbundle and restructure the publicly-owned power utility in 1998. It was first split into operating subsidiaries and then independent companies for generation (Central Electricity Generation Company, CEGCO), transmission and dispatch (National Electric Power Company, NEPCO), as well as two regional distribution companies (IDECO and EDECO). In mid-2000, consultants (financed through a USAID grant and administered by the World Bank) were advising the government (i) on the development of bulk electricity tariffs for sales from generators to NEPCO and from NEPCO to distribution companies and bulk consumers; (ii) the demarcation of asset boundaries, the compilation of an asset register, and asset valuation; (iii) the development of commercial arrangements to create profit centers; and (iv) the establishment of operating codes. A privatization strategy for the sector is to be prepared by 2001.

- The electricity sector law 13-1999 establishes an electricity regulatory commission, which will set tariffs and issue licenses for the generation, transmission and distribution of power. It also permits private participation in all three sub-sectors. Contrary to international best practice, however, the regulator will not be independent but chaired by the Minister of Energy and Mineral Resources. The government is aware of the shortcomings of the current legal and regulatory system, and wishes to improve on it.

- In August 2000, Jordan was negotiating the contract for its first IPP with the winning bidder, Belgium's Tractebel.[43] Unlike some other countries in the region, Jordan has well sequenced sector reforms, by largely overhauling the legal and regulatory framework prior to the introduction of IPPs. The build-own-operate (BOO) plant with a capacity of about 450 MW, will primarily serve the Amman region. Upon completion in 2004, it will represent about 30 percent of total capacity. At the moment, CEGCO has a generation market share of 95 percent, with the balance accounted for by autoproducers.

- Jordan is also one of the few MPs, where good sector statistics are available. NEPCO publishes a comprehensive annual report with a range of performance indicators (e.g. productivity per employee, total cost per kWh sold, return on assets, self financing ratio, generation and distribution losses, details on tariff structure) and financial statements (e.g. profits, break-down of expenses and accounts receivable, loan installments and interest payments, cash flow analysis).

Box 7: Energy and the Environment

In the MPs, like in most other countries, the energy sector is an important source of pollution. In developed countries, with their high-income levels and modern energy sectors, renewable energy and other high-tech solutions may be suitable instruments to reduce emission. In the majority of the MPs, however, the most effective and least costly strategy to reduce the environmental impact of the energy sector in the short and medium term, is to remove the enormous inefficiencies, which still characterize the industry. System losses (often around 20 percent) should be addressed through utility restructuring and the privatization of distribution companies. In generation, competition, private management, and unbundling will induce companies to maximize energy efficiency and invest in new technologies. Tariff reform and the elimination of subsidies will reveal true costs to all participants in energy markets and thus reduce wasteful over-consumption, which manifests itself in high energy use intensity and disproportionately high demand growth across the region. An example for the environmental benefits that liberalization can bring, is the UK. In the years following reforms, emission of CO_2 and NO_x were reduced by 40 percent and 50 percent respectively as privatized utilities replaced old coal-fired plants with new gas-fired ones. Besides the removal of sector inefficiencies through liberalization and privatization, the most effective mechanisms to reduce pollution are demand management programs, environmental standards (e.g. unleaded gasoline for vehicles, diesel and power plant fuel with low sulfur content, strict emission limits for plants in urban areas), pollution taxes, and a policy framework that encourages the use of renewables. Another powerful instrument to cut energy-induced pollution is the introduction of natural gas to replace oil and coal in power generation. Several MPs are pursuing such a strategy.

Note: The Bibliography contains a list with written and online sources for additional information on the subject.

EGYPT: *Reforms have been lop-sided, with significant private participation but little progress with the introduction of competition and regulation.*

Electricity

- In the late 1990s, Egypt began to restructure its power sector. Some of the measures, however, are not in line with international best practice and incompatible with the rules governing the EU internal market. A new sector law from February 1998 (No. 18-1998) removed restrictions to private participation in the power sector and merged the former eight

---

[43] MEED (11 August 2000)

public distribution companies with the seven power generation zones of the Egyptian Electricity Authority (EEA), to create seven regional generation and distribution companies.[44] EEA retains control of the country's transmission backbone. It is not entirely clear why Egypt chose a strategy of vertical integration, which is contrary to the international trend of unbundling.

- The seven integrated regional generation and distribution companies are now under the control of the EEA, which was supposed to prepare them for partial privatization. While the sale of state assets in the energy sector would have set a precedent in the region, the privatization strategy chosen had three important drawbacks. First, the sequencing of reforms was sub-optimal, since privatization would have preceded the introduction of competition and the reform of the regulatory framework (e.g. no clear separation of regulatory and operational functions, no independent regulator). Second, the privatization of a minority stake can help to attract private capital into the sector, but unless private investors have a majority of voting rights, corporate governance and thus the quality of management remains largely unaffected. Third, unlike a sale to a foreign strategic investor (which brings in management and sector expertise), a pure stock-market floatation has little impact on operational efficiency. In early 1999, EEA hired privatization consultants to evaluate assets, recommend percentages to be sold, advise on privatization modalities, and prepare the actual transaction. The privatization, however, was subsequently postponed indefinitely. While the exact reasons are not known, it appears that inadequacies of the regulatory framework deterred potential investors. In late-2000, the government announced the unbundling of generation and distribution, as well as the appointment of an energy regulator.

- The government has decided that all new generation capacity will be built by the private sector. EEA will act as wholesale purchaser under long-term power purchasing agreements and resell and transmit the electricity to the seven regional power companies. Law 100 of June 1996 modified Law 12 of 1976 (which established EEA) to allow private sector participation (construction, ownership, operation, and transfer) in power generation and other infrastructure projects.[45] Currently, power demand is increasing at an annual rate of around 8 percent and the energy ministry estimates a need for 9,300 MW of new capacity until 2010.

- In February 1998, Egypt's first BOT in Sidi Krir was awarded to a consortium headed by InterGen and Bechtel of the US. The main components of the package are a power purchasing agreement, a fuel supply agreement, a land-lease agreement, a Central Bank guarantee, and a turn-key construction contract. The 650-MW oil and gas fired plant, requiring investments of around $ 400 million, is scheduled to come on stream in 2001. Thanks to a highly transparent process, efficiently managed by international consultants, the demand for the tender was high (19 groups applied, 9 actually bid) and the winning bid of 2.6 c/kWh was one of the lowest ever achieved world-wide. This, however, appears to be partly due to a gas price in the fuel-supply agreement, which is below the world market (i.e. implicitly subsidized). The EEA subsequently replicated the IPP-model used in Sidi Krir for two more 650 MW-BOTs in Suez and East Port Said and recently launched tenders for two further IPPs, in which exchange rate risk was supposed to be transferred to the developer. The new BOT plants will operate with only one fifth of the staff employed by their public

---

[44] Like in several other southern Mediterranean countries, some municipalities buy bulk power from the public utility and distribute it independently within their area.

[45] Project Finance (August 1998)

sector equivalents.[46] Despite the success of these individual transactions, the strategy of introduction of IPPs prior to sector reforms, runs counter to the negative lessons learned by other countries.

- In recent years, Egypt has gradually increased electricity tariffs. While they are now closer to cost-recovery levels, hidden subsidies persist in the form of fuel costs below world market prices. Other problems undermine the financial viability of the electricity sector. System losses, for example, are estimated to be between 16 and 18 percent. Another structural issue are non-payments. At the end of fiscal year 1998/99 arrears of EEA amounted to $ 2.7 billion (much of which irrecoverable) or the equivalent of one year's revenues.

Box 8: The Benefits of Good Advice and Transparent Procedures

The successful outcome of the IPP tender in Sidi Krir provides two important lessons: the importance of hiring first-class consultants and the advantages of a transparent and well-managed tender process. Both general sector reforms and individual privatization transactions involve complex technical, legal, and financial issues. It is therefore critical that governments receive the best advice possible. Assistance from second-rate consultants is not only money wasted but usually leads to sub-optimal decisions. Given the high economic costs of such mistakes, it generally pays to hire top-notch advisors, even if they charge comparatively high fees. Following a number of disappointing privatization results in other sectors, for instance, the government of Egypt issued a policy statement in July 1998, declaring that international advisors would be involved in all future asset disposals. The willingness to pay for good advice, however, is not enough in itself. It is also important to carefully select consultants, to closely monitor their performance, and to set the right incentives.

A second lesson from Sidi Krir is the importance of a transparent and well-managed tender process (again, usually with the help of advisors) for privatizations, concessions, procurement contracts, or the award of subsidies (e.g. for renewable energy). This includes carefully prepared tender documents, international competitive bidding, a transparent process, as well as speedy but careful bid evaluation and contract negotiations. All this serves to lower transaction costs and increases investor interest. Egypt's Ministry for Electricity and Energy (MOEE) was widely praised for the well-managed process for the award of the Sidi Krir IPP (including its strategic use of top-notch international advisors) and subsequently invited by its Saudi counterparts to advise them on how to manage BOT tenders.

Natural Gas

- The Petroleum Ministry is systematically engaging the private sector for the exploration of Egypt's large natural gas reserves (an estimated 50 trillion cubic feet). In field development, foreign companies have committed to invest $ 2 billion in 1998-2000 alone. Domestic gas consumption is expected to increase dramatically over the coming years, as more and more power stations are gas-fired, several heavy industry projects come on stream, and private households are gradually being hooked up to new distribution networks.[47]

- The Investment & Incentives Law (No. 8-1997) opened the transport and distribution of gas to private investors.[48] In 1998, the Egyptian General Petroleum Corporation (EGPC) awarded a number of regional gas transmission and distribution franchises (BOTs) to areas that were previously without supply. In April 1998 the Nile Valley Gas Company, a consortium led by

---

[46] MEED (17 April 1998)
[47] MEED (3 October 1997 and 30 October 1998)
[48] MEED (13 February 1998)

Box 9: The Development and Regulation of New Gas Markets

Several of the MPs are in the process of developing or plan to develop downstream markets for natural gas – primarily to industrial customers (mainly power plants), but increasingly also for household consumption. It will be critical that governments develop a comprehensive energy sector strategy, instead of introducing gas in an ad hoc fashion. Given the interdependencies between power and gas markets (gas is a fuel for power plants but in some cases also a substitute for electricity), both markets should have a common regulatory framework and a common regulatory authority. The main policy challenge in new gas markets is to attract private investment for the construction of pipelines and distribution networks, without excessive restrictions on competition. If investors are to recoup their costs, however, they will generally need exclusivity rights for a limited period.

Even if high investment costs make the granting of limited monopoly rights necessary, some elements of competition can be introduced. First, in a larger country like Egypt, the granting of several regional licenses or concessions to different investors permits the introduction "yardstick competition". This means that the regulator can compare the performance of different local monopolies and that peer pressure gives companies an incentive to meet the highest standards. Second, by awarding a license or concession through an international competitive tender, the authorities can create "competition for the market" even when "competition in the market" is not feasible. As Egypt's IPP tender for Sidi Krir has shown, this forces companies to bid aggressively and will thus transfer most of the benefits associated with the monopoly rights to the government. Third, transparent regulation will help to prevent monopolistic abuses during the exclusivity period.

Besides Egypt, which has been a regional pioneer in the development of a downstream gas market, the experience of Northern Ireland offers some instructive lessons. Unlike the rest of the UK, Northern Ireland did not have a market for natural gas. In the mid-1990s Phoenix Natural Gas was granted an exclusive transport and supply license with detailed investment obligations, in order to ensure the construction of a well designed and extensive network. It was geographically confined to the greater Belfast area, where a high population density made the investments economically viable. In a mature gas market, transport and supply should be unbundled to increase competition, but in an emerging market a joint license is usually needed to ensure an integrated rollout of the infrastructure. The compromise used in Northern Ireland was to grant a combined license with separate accounts and different conditions for transport and supply. For transport, the exclusivity period was fixed at 20 years and transport charges were set at a level that should ensure a real pre-tax return of 8.5 percent over that period, based on forecasts for capital and operating expenses as well as demand. To reduce the uncertainty, a re-forecast will be made every five years and the regulator has been given some discretion to modify investment obligations. In supply, Phoenix will face competition after two to three years for industrial customers and from 2004 onwards for small users. This gives the operator an incentive to roll out the network quickly, to make full use of the exclusivity period. Given the competition between fuels, there is no price regulation for supply, although a provision in the concession contract would allow for it to be introduced after five years, if need be.

Another area, where MPs have attracted and plan to attract further private investments in downstream gas, are cross-border pipelines between gas producing and gas importing countries. Two pipelines already export gas from Algeria to Europe: Transmed through Tunisia to Italy and the Gazoduc Maghreb-Europe (GME) through Morocco to Spain and Portugal. Additional cross-border pipelines for the transport of natural gas which are under construction or being planned include those from Egypt to Jordan, Israel, and West Bank & Gaza, the one from Libya to Italy (to be completed by 2003), and a pipeline from Syria to Lebanon.

Note: The information on Northern Ireland was taken from the World Bank Viewpoint note "The Regulation of New Natural Gas Markets – The Northern Ireland Experience", by P. Lehmann (April 1998). For this and additional information on sector policies for the natural gas market, please refer to the Bibliography.

British Gas and Edison (both holding 37.5 percent, with the rest in the hands of local partners) was awarded a 25-year franchise. It grants exclusivity rights to supply industrial customers and households in Upper Egypt and will involve investments of around $ 220 million in four phases.[49] The franchise for Suez and part of Sinai was awarded to the ENI-led City Gas group in October 1998.[50] Two other franchises went to Egypt Gas (a listed joint venture majority owned by EGPC) for the Central Delta and to City Gas (in which ENI of Italy is the lead investor) for Suez.

- Within five years, Egypt plans to export a quarter of the gas it produces. Plans for a pipeline to Jordan were put on hold in 1999 following the discovery of reserves in Jordan. In October 1998, agreements were signed for the export of piped gas to West Bank & Gaza. As part of its domestic franchise, ENI is currently building a pipeline to El-Arish, close to Gaza and has long-term plans to supply Jordan and Israel with Egyptian gas. The gas would cost the Palestinian Authority about half of what is currently being charged by the Israel Electric Company. The company to be granted the import rights and the price to consumers has not yet been determined.[51] In December 1999, an agreement to build a pipeline from Egypt to Israel was announced, but might not materialize due to recent gas discoveries off the Israeli coast. In December 2000, a memorandum of understanding was signed for a $ 1 billion submarine pipeline for exports to Lebanon, Syria, Jordan, Turkey, and the EU.[52]

LEBANON: *Sector inefficiencies are imposing significant economic costs but reforms have made little progress to date.*

- A range of sector indicators illustrate the urgent need to increase technical and economic efficiency, as well as the financial sustainability of the power sector. Operational and investment subsidies from the government budget amounted to $ 480 million in 1996-98 and are expected to increase to $ 640 million in 1999-2002, despite the fact that electricity tariffs are high by international standards (an average of 8.6 c/kWh). System losses, both technical and particularly those due to unaccounted-for electricity, amounted to 44 percent of total power available from generation and imports. Cumulative arrears reached $ 360 million in 1998 (excluding irrecoverable receivables), or the equivalent of 310 days worth of revenue. In light of the alarming level of government debt, the 1999-2005 power investment program of $ 1 billion can only be financed if substantial private participation is introduced in the sector.

- Up to now, Lebanon's electricity sector remains largely unreformed. Electricité du Liban (EdL) is still a non-corporatized, vertically integrated, public monopoly with very weak commercial functions. There is no regulatory authority and the regulatory framework is rudimentary. The sector law dates from the early 1970s. Private participation has been confined to marginal functions and included management contracts for power plant operation and maintenance (O&M), outsourcing of meter reading and bill collection, some local distribution concessions, and hydro-plants. Capacity for regulation, policy formulation, and sector planning at the Ministry is very weak, reflecting the past focus on physical reconstruction.

---

[49] Financial Times (18 April 1998) and MEED (1 May 1998)
[50] MEED (30 October 1998)
[51] Financial Times (13 October 1998)
[52] Dow Jones International News Service (15 December 2000)

- The Lebanese Government is developing a reform strategy for the sector. According to the official presentation made at the Energy Forum in Granada (May 2000), the government plans to eliminate subsidies to EdL by 2001 and have all future generation capacity constructed by the private sector. The vertically integrated utility is to be unbundled into three subsidiaries for generation, transmission & dispatch, and distribution. Generation and distribution are to be privatized and liberalized. An independent regulator, the Higher Energy Council (HEC), is to be appointed and detailed sector regulations are to be drawn up.

- The general privatization law and the law that creates an Energy Ministry were passed in the spring of 2000. The draft electricity sector law, which provides for private participation, the unbundling of the sector, and the establishment of an autonomous regulator, has been approved by the Council of Ministers and awaits Parliamentary approval. In the fall of 2000, consultants were being mobilized to assist in the process of unbundling and privatization. Given the enormous system losses, the privatization of distribution is considered a priority.

- The World Bank and the European Commission have pledged significant technical assistance (TA) in the electricity sector. The World Bank has an on-going Power Sector Restructuring and Transmission project, which includes $ 6 million worth of TA. Under this project, it has helped the government to develop its sector strategy and is providing assistance for its implementation (e.g. review of the sector laws, capacity building at the Ministry and EdL). A Euro 30 million Meda project, the Investment Planning Program (IPP), consists of six project modules. It was approved in 1996 but due to delays on both sides, it has not yet been launched. In 1999, the EC-WB Programme on Private Participation in Mediterranean Infrastructure (PPMI) helped the EC and the government to restructure the two cross-sectoral IPP-modules for privatization and concessions, as well as the sector-specific one for the power sector. It is hoped that these projects will finally be launched in late 2000. As a joint program between the Commission and the World Bank, PPMI also helps to coordinate the interventions of both donors.

- Lebanon does not have any petroleum reserves and thus no sectors for upstream oil and gas. In downstream oil, the government plans to liberalize and privatize the import and distribution of petroleum products. The role of the public sector will be reduced to regulation and policy formulation. Another priority is to find a permanent solution for two state-owned refineries. They have been closed for years but still "employ" about 500 workers and represent a considerable drain on public finances. The government would also like to substitute oil for gas imports and is currently studying the possibility of constructing a transmission pipeline to Syria or a terminal for LNG imports.

ISRAEL: *Sector reforms have begun but political resistance and lack of regional interconnection remain structural obstacles.*

- *The Israel Electric Company (IEC) is a state-owned and vertically integrated power monopoly.* The influential IEC trade unions have successfully resisted past attempts by the government to break up the monopoly and to reduce the unusually generous privileges of workers, which include free electricity for employees. Nonetheless, the outgoing CEO of IEC managed to introduce some less contentious, but equally important reforms. The utility considerably improved customer services and established a popular call center. Thanks to massive investments in distribution, power outages were reduced by 40 percent from 350 minutes in 1996 to 207 minutes in 1999. The conversion of oil-fired power stations to natural gas was completed and helped to further enhance efficiency.

- A new 1996 electricity law stipulates that the generation sector is to be gradually opened to competition (starting with 10 percent of total generation capacity), through the introduction of private independent power plants. Unlike in the case of other IPPs in the region, the government wants to see private generators compete with the incumbent, by selling directly to customers. At the same time, the state utility began to operate under a 10-year license to enhance the transparency of the regulatory framework and to strengthen regulatory control.[53] Despite resistance from the EIC, the government also plans to unbundle and partly privatize the sector.

Box 10: Policy Reform and Utility Restructuring

The restructuring of energy companies has to be an integral part of broader sector reform. Policy changes at the sector level need to be implemented at the utility level to become effective. Electricity unbundling for instance, involves not only policy measures (e.g. a new sector law and an independent regulator) but also company restructuring (e.g. the separation of accounts, the corporatization of the resulting entities, or the establishment of transaction mechanisms between generation, transmission and distribution). Even though the nature and extent of restructuring needs vary across the region, most of the state-owned enterprises (SOEs) in the electricity sector are in significant need of restructuring, including:

- the transfer of all regulatory (as opposed to operational) functions from the utility to the sector regulator or the Ministry;
- corporatization (i.e. organized under company law with proper accounts etc.);
- the unbundling of generation, transmission, distribution (e.g. separation of accounts, allocation of assets and staff, creation of independent institutional structures and legal entities);
- the commercialization and financial restructuring of these entities (e.g. strengthening of commercial functions in terms of processes and resources, balance-sheet restructuring, tariff-rebalancing, staffing reforms);
- in distribution and sales, the set-up of effective metering, billing, and customer relations systems (e.g. reform of metering and billing procedures, installation of a customer database);
- for transmission and dispatch, the creation of effective market structures (e.g. contractual arrangements with generation and distribution companies, network control and management);
- for generation, introduction of state-of-the-art plant management and technology;
- the preparation and implementation of alliances, mergers and acquisitions, and privatization;
- general training of managerial, commercial, and engineering staff; and
- the installation of IT-systems, new processes, and organizational structures.

- The Government instructed IEC to add 900 MW of additional generation capacity through IPPs by 2005. The first IPP contract for the 370 MW CCGT at Ramat Hovav was concluded in 1997. IEC, which ran the tender process, included a clause obliging the developer to sell power exclusively to itself. In April 1999, Israel's anti-trust authority ruled this clause to be illegal, since it ran counter to sector legislation enacted to introduce competition.[54] These

---

[53] Haaretz Newspaper (3 May 2000)
[54] Like in most countries of the EU, the energy sector is being regulated both by a sector authority (the Public Utilities Authority) and the general competition authority.

legal complications delayed the Ramat Hovav project as well as other planned IPPs by at least two years.[56]

- A rapid rise in electricity consumption has resulted in a fall in reserve capacity from 25 to around 10 percent over the last decade. 25 percent is considered the minimum safety level, since Israel is not interconnected to the grids of its neighbors. The government hopes to reach an agreement on interconnections with Egypt, Jordan, and possibly the Palestinian Authority, should the latter build its own power plant in Gaza. This would permit the country to reduce its inefficiently high reserve margin requirements (see also Section 4.3 on interconnections and power trade in the region).

- Two exploration consortia have recently discovered a natural gas field off the Israeli coast. The estimated 45 billion m^3 could cover the country's energy needs for up to 15 years. Nonetheless, Israel is also considering to import gas through a pipeline from Egypt. The government intends to introduce competition in downstream gas market right from the beginning, by separating the supply (2 offshore licenses) from the actual transport of gas.[57]

WEST BANK AND GAZA: A *small market and territorial fragmentation call for greater regional integration.*

- The Palestinian Energy Authority faces not only the typical problems associated with small systems, but also additional obstacles resulting from fragmentation of its service area and its dependence on the Israel Electric Company. West Bank and Gaza currently has no own power plants but imports up to 300 MW (95 percent of all power) from Israel at a high price of 7 c/kWh. Per capita power consumption is low by regional standards and expected to increase. In 1997, the Palestinian Energy Authority (PEA) established the Palestinian Electricity Company (PEC), which raised about $ 20 million through an IPO on the Palestinian Securities Exchange in mid-2000.[58] PEA has also signed a 20-year concession for an IPP in the Gaza Strip, which will start operation with 80 MW and could be expanded to a capacity of 215 MW. It is expected to come on stream in late 2000 and will supply power at 4.7 c/kWh. The plant will use gas from Egypt and should allow Gaza to become self-sufficient with regard to electricity.

- Distribution networks in West Bank and Gaza have traditionally been managed by the municipalities. They buy power from the IEC and re-sell it to final customers with a substantial mark-up to finance municipal services. Due to poor maintenance, assets have deteriorated considerably over recent years and the PEA estimates rehabilitation needs to be around $ 130 million (in May 1998, the EIB approved a loan of $ 39 million). Given the small size and technical isolation of distribution networks, there are plans to connect and organizationally merge local networks into one distribution company for Gaza and three for the West Bank (north, south, and center) in order to increase technical and operational efficiency.

- The PEA is also considering the creation of a Palestinian Grid Company, possibly with private participation, to upgrade the back-bone system, manage transmission and dispatch,

---

[56] Haaretz Newspaper (2 and 10 August 2000)
[57] Financial Times (7 September 2000)
[58] The Jerusalem Post (5 September 2000)

and implement further links to neighboring countries. Interconnections to Egypt and Jordan, as well as further integration with the Israeli network could considerably increase efficiency (e.g. competition between suppliers, lower reserve capacity, higher system integrity). As discussed in Section 4.3, it could be a central component in a more ambitious scheme of interconnecting national grids throughout the Middle East. Contrasting the unique challenges the authorities in West Bank & Gaza were facing, the Palestinian delegation made an interesting remark at the May 2000 Energy Forum. They found it extremely difficult to build a power infrastructure from scratch but considered themselves lucky to be able to build a legal and institutional sector framework from scratch—rather than converting an existing one in the face of "people's natural resistance to change".

Box 11: Tariffs and Subsidies

As prices in any market, energy tariffs influence the decisions and behavior of suppliers, investors, and consumers. They are an important instrument for economic resource allocation and the pursuit of sector efficiency. A number of pricing principles govern the EU Single Market and are enshrined in the EU's competition and state aid rules, as well as other parts of the acquis communautaire. They include the following: First, where competition is feasible, prices should be determined by market mechanisms. Price competition induces energy companies to cut costs and to pass on efficiency improvements to their customers. Second, in monopolistic market segments (e.g. power transmission and distribution), a degree of regulation is generally needed to prevent monopolistic pricing. This, however, should be transparent and well targeted. Third, economic efficiency requires that energy prices reflect economic costs (i.e. full cost recovery of energy companies and pollution taxes to take account of environmental costs). Prices should neither be artificially low as a result of open or hidden (cross-)subsidies, nor excessively high because of monopoly rents. Fourth, price increases resulting from scarcity (e.g. too little generation or transmission capacity) should provide signals to investors of where new infrastructure is needed and at the same time, permit them to generate a fair return on investments.

Throughout the southern Mediterranean, tariff reforms should be an integral part of energy sector reform. Liberalization should introduce market mechanisms needed to determine efficient prices. In many MPs, energy prices are still below cost-recovery levels and tariff-rebalancing is needed. General price subsidies (which often favor higher income groups with higher energy consumption) should be replaced by more targeted and less distortive assistance to the poor. Where needed, carefully designed pollution taxes should be levied.

SYRIA: *An outdated sector framework and lack of tariff reform preclude private investment.*

- The energy sector remains entirely state-owned and operated by public entities, while competition is non-existent. Sector data is difficult to find, but efficiency seems to be low. System losses, for instance, are estimated to be as high as 25 percent.[58] As in most other countries of the region, significant increases in electricity demand will create the need for significant additional generation capacity over the coming decade.

- The Government follows a policy of "controlled" energy prices. Energy tariffs are administratively established and generally subsidized. This is particularly true for electricity,

---

[58] US Energy Information Administration (March 2000)

where prices are well below economic cost. The average electricity tariff is about 2.6 c/kWh, compared to production cost of about 8 c/kWh.

- Until electricity tariffs are raised to cost-recovery levels and other reforms are instituted, Syria will have difficulties to attract private operators and investors. Syria remains an example of the Phase II model of sector organization (see Section 1.2), with the Government as the source of capital and the costs of inefficiencies borne by taxpayers.

MOROCCO: *An effective state-owned utility and large private investments contrast with the absence of competition and an outdated regulatory regime.*

- As the vertically integrated and non-corporatized state monopoly, the Office National de l'Electricité (ONE) continues to dominate the sector. There is no independent sector regulator and practically no competition within the industry. Morocco has opted for the single buyer model, whereby ONE has a monopoly to purchase power from all IPPs through PPAs and controls the transmission network. 11 municipal régies, which have exclusivity rights for the distribution and re-sale within their respective areas (local retail monopolies), buy wholesale power directly from ONE (wholesale monopoly). By law, ONE retains the right of ownership for all generation assets over 10 MW. This also applies to IPPs, where investment and management are contracted out to the private sector. In summary, competition and regulation in the Moroccan power market are weak, but the state-owned utility is generally well managed and regarded as efficient by international standards.

- Morocco was the first country in North Africa to introduce IPPs. At a total cost of about $ 1.5 billion, Morocco's 1,350 MW power project in Jorf Lasfar is the largest independent power facility in the region. Located 130 km south of Casablanca, it will eventually generate one third of Morocco's power supply and is the country's biggest foreign investment ever. In late 1997, and after extensive negotiations, the 30-year BOT contract between the Moroccan government and a joint venture of the Swedish-Swiss ABB and CMS Energy of the US was concluded. The complex package includes the construction of two units with a total capacity of 696 MW, as well as the transfer (privatization) of two existing plants with 660 MW from ONE. Other elements of the deal are a concession to operate the coal terminal of the Jorf Lasfar port and a 30-year power-purchasing agreement with ONE. Although this project mobilized significant investments and has improved operational efficiency in power generation, it poses several obstacles to future reform. On the one hand, Jorf Lasfar's large market share will make it difficult to establish a market in generation. On the other hand, the long duration of the PPA could leave ONE (and thus the government) with significant liabilities (stranded costs), if future competition reduces retail prices to levels below those fixed in the PPA.

- The privatization of distribution is also relatively well advanced. So far, two of the largest régies, Casablanca and Rabat, have been concessioned to private companies, with the involvement of foreign investors. In 1997, Lyonnaise des Eaux signed a long-term concession to operate distribution in Casablanca (for electricity and water/sewage combined). In 1998 a consortium led by Spanish and Portuguese investors won a similar contract for Rabat, making investment commitments of $ 1.3 billion. Two similar deals for Tangier and Tetouan, involving investment commitments of $ 1 billion, were to be concluded by early 2001. In principle, the privatization of distribution networks in Morocco could be a precedent for similar moves in other MPs. However, two problems with the chosen scheme should be highlighted. First, the fact that the Casablanca and Rabat concessions were awarded through exclusive negotiations and not through a competitive tender, probably led to a sub-optimal outcome. Second, due to the long term nature and type of contracts signed, the scope for future sector reform has been reduced—in particular with respect to the unbundling of distribution infrastructure and supply (trade) as well as the right of the distributors to by power from other generator besides ONE.

- A 1999 World Bank study, funded by a Japanese grant and commissioned by the government, analyzed Morocco's options for the gradual introduction of competition in the power sector, while taking account of the above-mentioned constraints. It proposed a three-phase action plan. During Phase I (2002-2004), ONE would be unbundled and remaining generation and distribution functions spun off with the involvement of private investors. Detailed regulations would be developed and ONE left with the management of the transmission grid. It would acquire the institutional structures and capacity needed for system management in an unbundled environment. Phase II (2005 to 2012) would start with a market review, on the basis of which competition would be introduced to the extent possible, while leaving a sufficiently large captive market for the IPP operators to recoup stranded costs. The main objective during Phase III (2012 to 2015), would be to establish a genuine wholesale market and to grant all customers (with the exception of households) the freedom to chose their supplier.

- Morocco is the only MP where network expansion is a major policy issue in the sector. Currently, a mere 15 percent of Morocco's large rural population (and 46 percent of the total) has access to electricity. In June 1999, ONE announced an ambitious investment plan for rural electrification. Another project under preparation are the Tangier and Tarfaya wind farms, with a total capacity of 200 MW. The $ 200 million needed are to be raised through a BOT scheme. A similar 50 MW scheme, funded by EdF and other investors, is already in operation near Tétouan. At the time of writing, the World Bank was assisting the Moroccan government in carrying out a global environmental study for the energy sector.

- Morocco is interconnected to its neighbors Spain and Algeria and there is substantial potential for greater cross-border integration of its power market. A 400 kV interconnector with Spain is already being used to import both baseload supply (up to 90 MW) and peak supply (up to 200 MW) from the Spanish spot market, where ONE has a license to trade. As an illustrative example for the benefits of trade, Morocco can thus import power at competitive prices of 2-3 c/kWh, compared to the domestic generation costs of about 4-5 c/kWh. Morocco also has the right to purchase 600 million m^3 of natural gas per year from Algeria through the GME gas pipeline (which crosses Morocco on its way to Spain). This may be used to fuel the future IPP-type plant in Tahaddart.

TUNISIA: *Sector efficiency is high but policy reforms are at an early stage.*

- The public utility Société Tunisienne de l'Electricité et du Gaz (STEG) is a vertically integrated monopoly for power and gas. According to the IXth development plan (1997-2001), energy tariffs were supposed to be brought closer in line with costs and STEG was to be split into two separate companies for power and gas. This, however, has not yet happened and the government has no plans to unbundle the two or to increase competition.

- Private participation is currently confined to the contracting out of certain services (e.g. 80 percent of meter installations work), to autoproduction (up to 40 MW) and to one IPP. A 470 MW BOO power plant in Radès, involving investments of about $ 250 million, will add 25 percent to the country's total generating capacity. After Decree No. 96-1125 of June 1996 opened the sector for private concessions, a transparent, open, and competitive bidding process led to an award of the IPP to a US-Japanese consortium. The subsequent negotiations, however took 2.5 years and financial closure was only reached in June 1999. Due to more advanced technology and higher operational efficiency, it has been estimated that the IPP could produce power at a bulk cost (excluding fuel) 20 percent lower than plants currently operated by STEG.

Diagram 8: Electricity Prices in Selected MPs

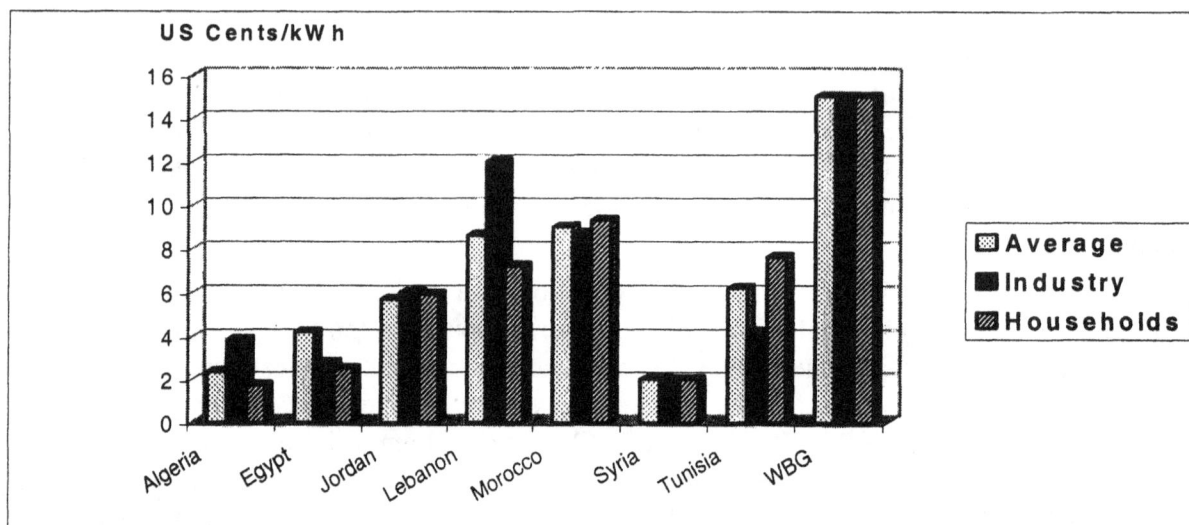

Source: World Bank.

ALGERIA: *The Government has ambitious plans to overhaul the energy sector and introduce greater private participation.*

Electricity

- To date, the electricity sector in Algeria remains largely unreformed. The vertically integrated state-monopoly Sonelgaz it not yet corporatized. Government subsidies to the utility amounted to about $ 1 billion in 1998 alone. Separate accounts and departments for generation, transmission, and distribution have been created, but to date no separate legal entities have been established. There is neither competition nor private participation in any part of the power sector.

- The main function of the National Council of Energy (NCE) is to award and monitor exploration licenses in the upstream oil and gas sector, not to oversee the economic regulation of the power sector. It is separate from the Ministry of Energy and Mines and its members are appointed by the President.

- A new electricity law is expected to be passed by parliament by the end of 2000. It would unbundle and corporatize Sonelgaz, permit private participation (in generation only), and create separate energy (electricity and gas) and mining regulators. The transmission company would be the sole off-taker of power generated in the country.

- In July 2000, Sonelgaz issued an invitation for BOO power plants with a total capacity of up to 2000 MW. However, "international power executives expressed skepticism about the invitation. At a meeting called by Sonelgaz in late July, they told the company that clarification and greater detail were required before they could seriously consider applying for the project."[59] An ongoing effort to win investor interest for a 1,200 MW IPP in Hadjret En Nouss has not yet born fruit, partly due to uncertainties surrounding the future of the legal and regulatory framework.

Oil and Gas

- Together with Egypt, Algeria is the only MP with large oil and gas reserves. More than 95 percent of the country's exports are petrochemicals and most of these (e.g. 90 percent of crude oil exports) go to Europe. The industry continues to be dominated by the state oil company Sonatrach, which has signed more than 20 exploration and production sharing agreements with foreign companies.[60] The new government has expressed the intention to transfer responsibility for regulation and negotiations with investors to the ministry and eventually have Sonatrach compete for new projects with private companies.

- Two pipelines export natural gas from Algeria to Europe and the country supplies 12 percent of the EU's gas market. The Transmed pipeline runs through Tunisia to Italy and has a capacity of 30 billion m^3 per year. The new Gazoduc Maghreb-Europe (GME) is 1600 km long and passes through Morocco to Spain, with an extension to Portugal. Sonatrach and the main Spanish off-taker Enagas financed the construction costs of $ 2.5 billion. By 2001, it will reach an annual capacity of 20 billion m^3.

- In the main cities, about one million consumers are connected to a distribution network for natural gas. It is currently operated by a department of Sonelgaz, which is to become independent once the new sector law has been passed. There are plans to double the size of the network, but none for private participation in downstream gas.

---

[59] MEED (11 August 2000)
[60] "The Euro-Mediterranean Energy Partnership" by Debra Johnson, Financial Times Energy (June 2000)

Box 12:   WTO, GATT, and GATS

Whereas energy sector reforms at the national and regional level are discussed throughout this document, competition and private participation are also increasingly being driven through multilateral initiatives under the auspices of the World Trade Organization (WTO). The energy sector is both subject to the General Agreement on Tariffs and Trade (GATT) and the General Agreement on Trade in Services (GATS). Unlike trade in goods (covered under GATT), trade in services (subject to GATS) includes the cross-border movement of the factors of production (capital and labor). In the case of energy services, foreign direct investment is therefore considered part of international trade. Due to the unbundling of electricity and downstream gas, the distinction between energy goods and energy services has recently become more important. Whereas vertically integrated utilities previously covered the entire value-added chain (and thus services were only implicitly embedded in energy goods), unbundling has separated goods (e.g. generation and network infrastructure) from services (e.g. transport and distribution of power). Transportation and distribution of energy are considered as services under GATS, if provided independently.

"The cross-border trade of energy goods encounters obstacles such as tariffs, non-tariff barriers, and restrictive business practices (RBPs), such as the vertical foreclosure of transmission and distribution networks in the destination country. The WTO goods agreements deal with the first type of obstacles, while the second type (RBPs) falls out of the scope of WTO agreements, at least for the time being. [...] Cross-border trade in energy services encounters market access, national treatment, and other regulatory barriers and restrictive business practices by incumbent operators controlling transmission and distribution networks. All Members are bound by the GATS most favored nation (MFN) unconditional obligation while market access and national treatment barriers are dealt with by Articles XVI and XVII and by the progressive negotiations of specific commitments. Other domestic regulatory barriers are subject to the provisions of Article VI, including a test of necessity linking them to the policy objectives they are meant to serve. RBPs by incumbent operators are subject to Article VIII (rules on monopolies and exclusive services suppliers)." Article VIII implies that incumbents in the power and gas market may not discriminate against foreign companies and are prohibited from abusing their monopoly power in markets outside the scope of their monopoly.

Currently, international trade rules liberalize cross-border freedom of investment and market access (i.e. competition) only for small parts of the energy sector, mainly energy equipment. Energy goods and even more so energy services have long been outside the scope of GATT rules. This however, could soon change, as international liberalization of the energy sector progresses, preparations for a new global trade round on services are under way, and efforts are being made to more systematically tackle RBPs within GATT/GATS. These developments could also have implications for the Euro-Mediterranean Energy Partnership. The European Commission (which has a mandate to negotiate trade issues on behalf of all 15 EU Member States) has traditionally played a key role in the GATT/GATS process. Of the 12 MPs, 8 (Cyprus, Egypt, Israel, Malta, Morocco, Tunisia, Turkey, and since 2000 Jordan) are WTO members, and others may follow.

Source: "Energy Services", WTO (1998)

Chapter 4

The Way Forward:

National Reforms and Regional Initiatives

4 THE WAY FORWARD:
NATIONAL REFORMS AND REGIONAL INITIATIVES

4.1 Introduction

At the national level, each Mediterranean Partner (MP) will have to reform its sector framework and restructure its energy utilities. As the experience in other countries has shown, developing and implementing a comprehensive reform strategy requires political leadership, an ability to build consensus, and the determination to overcome technical and political obstacles on the way. Each of the MPs is ultimately responsible for its own domestic reforms, but technical assistance from donors and the framework of the Euro-Mediterranean Energy Partnership may provide useful support. Several assistance instruments are available for this purpose and it is important that they are used in a complementary fashion:

- *The Energy Forum and its three Ad-hoc Groups* on Energy Policy, Economic Analysis, and Interconnections permit policy-makers and sector experts from the various Euro-Med countries to exchange experience and coordinate reforms.

- *Regional Meda Projects* should provide analytic inputs (research, reports) and logistical support (organization of conferences, training modules, study tours) for this policy dialogue.

- *National projects*, sponsored by the EC, the World Bank or other donors should be used to provide in-depth technical assistance and training to prepare and implement national reforms. Experience from national projects should be fed back into regional initiatives and regional initiatives should be used to facilitate national projects.

- Another, potentially powerful instrument to support reforms at the country-level are *sectoral adjustment operations* supported by the World Bank, European Commission and other donors. These require careful preparation and should only be used, once a government has developed a coherent reform strategy.

In principle, the Euro-Mediterranean Energy Partnership could deal with a large number of issues (e.g. security of supply, environment, liberalization, interconnections) as well as various sub-sectors (power, upstream and downstream oil and gas). Given limited resources and capacity, however, governments and donors need to establish priorities. They should concentrate on those initiatives with the highest payoffs. The central element of the Euro-Mediterranean Partnership is the creation of the Euro-Mediterranean free-trade area and the purpose of the Meda program is to facilitate the economic and social adjustment it entails. The natural priorities for the Energy Partnership are therefore sector reform and the cross-border integration of energy markets. This would be particularly timely, since the EU is implementing similar reforms internally.

The Role of the Commission and EIB

As discussed at length in Chapter 2, the Commission's Directorate General for Transport and Energy (DG TREN) has been driving reforms within the EU single market and should feed its EU-internal experience and technical expertise more systematically into the Euro-Mediterranean Energy Partnership. To date, this potential remains under-exploited, partly due to the fact that the ongoing sector reforms within the EU and the accession candidate countries fully absorb institutional resources. DG TREN has a Unit dedicated to cooperation with non-EU countries, which deals both with the accession countries and with the Mediterranean Partners. This should make it easier to transfer experience between these two neighboring regions of the EU.

According to the traditional division of labor between the Commission and the *European Investment Bank* (EIB), the EC deals with infrastructure sector policies, while the EIB finances physical infrastructure within the EU and in selected partner countries. The EIB is therefore not well placed to help the southern Mediterranean countries in the modernization of their policy framework (the EC would be the appropriate partner for this)—but it may contribute to national investment projects, as well as to the financing of interconnection projects and thus the regional integration of energy markets.

The Role of the World Bank

The traditional strengths of the World Bank are its global expertise in energy sector reform as well as its experience in policy analysis and policy advice. It has well-developed knowledge-management structures, publishes extensively on energy policy issues (see Bibliography), and has both regional and global sector teams that can be mobilized to assist client governments in the region on a wide range of issues. The World Bank is providing extensive policy advice throughout the Central and Eastern European accession countries, as well as in most countries of the southern Mediterranean (Jordan, Lebanon, Morocco, Turkey, West Bank & Gaza). The Euro-Mediterranean Partners might want to draw these resources more systematically into the adjustment process, as has been done in the EU accession countries (see Box 13 below). As discussed in the Foreword, the joint WB-EC Programme on Private Participation in Mediterranean Infrastructure (PPMI), based in Brussels, continues to be available to facilitate cooperation between its two parent institutions.

The Role of Energy Companies

If the modernization of sector frameworks is to be successful, formerly state-owned and vertically integrated utilities will have to be restructured (see Section 2.5). At the same time—and as the experience of Latin America, the EU and other regions has shown—liberalization and privatization are needed to create adjustment pressure at the utility level. Assistance for company restructuring can come from a variety of sources:

- The regional Meda energy project for "Restructuring of Energy Companies", expected to be launched in late-2000, will organize training modules and workshops to help utilities in the MPs in the adjustment process.

- Given the significant technical assistance needs, however additional national projects, sponsored by the EC, the World Bank, or other donors, should be identified.

- Both national and regional projects should be designed to involve sector federations within the EU. The Union of the Electricity Industry (EURELECTRIC), the European Federation of Transmission System Operators (ETSO), the European Federation of Energy Traders (EFET) and others should be tapped for expertise, training material, and contacts (see Chapter 2).

- Direct cooperation between southern Mediterranean utilities and foreign companies could also play an important role in the restructuring of MP energy companies. The most powerful instrument to achieve the transfer of managerial and technical expertise would be the partial or complete sale to a foreign strategic investor. Twinning arrangements without equity participation tend to be less effective.

Box 13: WB-EC Cooperation in the Accession Countries

In preparation of EU accession, the countries of Central and Eastern Europe (CEE), as well as Turkey, Cyprus, and Malta, have launched ambitious programs of economic adjustment. Energy is one of the sectors in which they have to transpose the *acquis communautaire* and prepare their industries for the competition and opportunities arising from a common market (see section 2.6). Although the reform process is largely driven by the countries themselves, many of them have requested technical assistance (TA) from donors. At a joint World Bank–European Commission energy workshop in Brussels in 1998, both organizations agreed to use the accession candidates as a test case for closer donor coordination in the sector. The idea was to combine the strength of the Commission (detailed knowledge of the EU Single Market for energy) with those of the World Bank (global experience in energy sector reforms) to the benefit of the transition countries.

One of the first initiatives was the launch of a series of multilateral *workshops* to familiarize top-level officials from the accession candidate countries with key elements of reform. At the time of writing, workshops had been held on the 'implementation of the Internal Market Directive for Electricity', the 'implementation of the Internal Market Directive for Gas', and on 'regulation in the energy sector'. A fourth workshop on TSOs took place in June 2000, with the support of EURELECTRIC, and others will follow. The same format is being used in all the events: both organizations share the costs; outside institutions are hired to prepare documentation (e.g. the Dutch university of Leiden for the workshop on regulation); the Commission presents the EU experience; and the World Bank contributes case studies of other developing countries as well as global best practice in sector reform. According to the organizers, the most important result of the workshops turned out to be the contacts between the officials from different countries. They proactively shared their positive and negative experiences and kept in touch after the events. Through these exchanges, countries which had been more cautious in their restructuring were encouraged to accelerate their reforms after seeing what others have achieved.

To deepen the process initiated through the workshops, the WB and EC have conducted *joint missions* to all of the thirteen accession candidates, except for Bulgaria, Cyprus, and Malta (latter two are not eligible for WB loans). The main purpose of these missions is to assess reform and TA needs in the individual countries and to help governments develop and implement sector strategies. Another useful TA instrument are *study tours*, like a recent visit of the Hungarian regulator to his Portuguese counterpart to exchange experience. Probably the most important contribution of the World Bank to the preparations for EU accession, however, is its *project work*. In most of the accession countries it has implemented or is still implementing projects in support of sector reform and it systematically integrates accession requirements into its project design. One of the areas where improvements would still be possible is in the closer integration of accession negotiations, led by DG TREN, with Phare projects (the CEE equivalent of Meda), which are prepared by DG Enlargement. Another one would be closer donor coordination with other International Finance Institutions (IFIs), like the European Investment Bank (EIB), the European Bank for Reconstruction and Development (EBRD), and the International Monetary Fund (IMF).

4.2 Regional and National Projects

Regional Meda Projects for Sector Restructuring

Three regional Meda energy projects, providing technical assistance for sector reform, are to be launched by the end of 2000. The projects "Support of the Three Ad-Hoc Groups of the Energy Forum", the "Reform of the Legal and Institutional Energy Sector Framework", and the "Restructuring of Energy Companies" will provide Euro 6.5 million worth of technical assistance. Through conferences, seminars, training modules, and research, they will help to build capacity, formulate sector policy, and disseminate best practice. The two projects "Reform of the Legal and Institutional Sector Framework" and "Restructuring of Energy Companies" will provide complementary assistance at the sector and the utility level. The results of both should feed into the project "Support to the Three Ad-Hoc Groups of the Energy Forum", which will give both substantive and logistical support to the Ad-hoc Groups (see next section). While the project consultants are to provide services, it is up to the MPs to make full use of them.

The Energy Forum and its Ad-Hoc Groups

Until recently, sector reforms did not feature prominently in the discussions of the Energy Forum. The imminent launch of the three Ad-Hoc Groups for Energy Policy, Economic Analysis, and Interconnections as well as that of the three regional Meda energy projects outlined above, provide an opportunity to re-focus the dialogue. In fact, the last Energy Forum, held in Granada (Spain) in May 2000, was the first one specifically devoted to policy reform. Representatives from the individual MPs discussed the current sector framework and future reform plans of their respective governments. Representatives from the European Commission and the World Bank, the President of the Council of European Energy Regulators, and other speakers discussed ongoing reforms in EU markets and global trends. Industry representatives explained how they were coping with sector adjustment and how policy makers could provide a more conducive sector framework. The Commission asked all MPs, to designate counterparts for the three Ad-Hoc Groups, which it would like to launch in late 2000 or early 2001.

National Reforms, TA Projects, and Sectoral Adjustment

Although regional Meda projects and the Energy Forum might be useful catalysts, they cannot be substitutes for a coherent government strategy and substantive sector reforms at the national level. National World Bank and Meda projects should be identified to mobilize the required technical assistance at the country level. This would require energy ministries to make a case and ensure their projects are included in the National Indicative Programs, agreed upon by their governments and the EC, and in the lending program of the World Bank. As the name "Mesures d'Accompagnement" underlines, the purpose of the Meda program is to support the process of social and economic transition. In fact the energy sector was one of the priority sectors identified in the Barcelona Declaration. In the past five years, however, the only country in the Maghreb and Mashrek region, which demanded funding for energy sector reform from the EC, was Lebanon. And even in this case, the project has been under preparation for more than three years, due to repeated delays on both sides. Under Meda II, the Commission and the southern Mediterranean countries should redouble their efforts to carefully prepare and speedily implement national Meda projects in support of sector reform. The World Bank has is also gearing up to increase its support to energy sector restructuring throughout the region.

Box 14:   Private Investment, Risk, and Public Sector Guarantees

One request that has occasionally been raised in the context of the Euro-Mediterranean Energy Forum, is the provision of guarantees by the European Commission and MP governments for private investments in the energy sector. This, however, would be undesirable and has rightfully been dismissed by the EC. Guarantees are a mechanism to transfer risk. The long-term power-purchasing agreements and fuel-supply agreements between private investors and public energy companies— commonly used for IPPs—are also implicit government guarantees, since they transfer currency and demand risks from the private to the public sector. Although explicit and implicit guarantees increase certainty for investors, their flip-side is that the public sector takes on large contingent liabilities. This means that taxpayers will have to foot the bill if problems arise. Whatever instrument is being used to transfer risk, economic efficiency requires that the party best suited to reduce risk should bear it. The private sector is not only used to taking risk (in fact this is one of its main functions) but also has a much better track-record of managing risk than the public sector. The main exception is political and regulatory risk (i.e. uncertainty resulting from government activity), which actually tends to be high in the energy sectors of many of the MPs.

The most effective mechanism to reduce regulatory risk, however, is not the provision of government guarantees but sector reforms that create a transparent, coherent, and stable regulatory framework. A modern sector law, for instance, removes legal ambiguities. A strong independent regulator with a clear mandate reduces political discretion and thus the risk of interference. Full (instead of partial) privatization can lend comfort to strategic foreign investors by reducing government control over a utility they invest in. The absence of a stable regulatory framework and the declared intention to maintain a strong government stake seem to have been the main reasons why the planned privatization of Egypt's regional generation and distribution companies did not attract sufficient investor interest. Legal provisions for international arbitration are another powerful instrument to reduce risk. As discussed above, Turkey changed its constitution in early 2000 to permit for it. Another important tool to create a more conducive environment for investments could be cross-border cooperation in the southern Mediterranean countries. Investors prefer large markets (economies of scale and risk diversification) and regional integration could help many of the small MPs to increase the size or their energy markets. A cross-border harmonization of regulatory frameworks (guided by the rules of the EU Single Market for energy), could be another alternative to guarantees. Minimizing political and regulatory risk reduces the cost of capital to potential investors and further encourages competition between them, thus lowering prices to consumers.

As the representative from the Spanish federation of energy companies UNESA explained at the Granada Energy Forum, the main reason why Spanish energy companies are investing heavily in Latin America but much less so in their neighboring region, is that Latin American countries have spent the past decade modernizing their regulatory regimes and creating competitive markets. MP governments and donors should focus on sector reform, if they wanted to attract more foreign direct investment (FDI) to the region. Should investors need guarantees nonetheless, they are readily available from a variety of sources. The World Bank Group, for instance, offers a variety of guarantees and related instruments: The International Finance Corporation (IFC, the WBG's private sector branch), Multilateral Investment Guarantee Agency (MIGA, the WBG's agency for investment guarantees against non-commercial risks), or the International Centre for the Settlement of Investment Disputes (ICSID, a WBG organization arbitrating between governments and private investors). As discussed in Box 15 below, accession to the *Energy Charter Treaty* could be another useful instrument to reduce investor risk.

One of the potentially most effective instruments of donor support to energy reform at the national level are sectoral adjustment operations. To successfully carry out such an operation, however, several preconditions have to be met. It is critical that the government has a well-developed sector strategy and the political will to implement it. On the donor side, a thorough understanding of the sector is needed. This will require significant prior research and preferably past involvement in the sector. At the same time, the donor will need to be able to deploy top-notch sector experts. Given the size of these interventions, poor or even mediocre advice could waste significant amounts of money or lead to sub-optimal policies that do more harm than good. Sectoral adjustment operations lend themselves well to donor co-financing. In the southern Mediterranean, the European Commission and the World Bank have a good track record of cooperation on structural adjustment. Should they decide to support sectoral adjustment in the energy sector, the joint WB-EC Programme on Private Participation in Mediterranean Infrastructure could provide technical inputs, as it is currently doing in the ongoing telecom adjustment operation in Morocco: two sectoral adjustment operations (one under preparation at the time of writing), combined with TA and an intensive policy dialogue, have accompanied the enactment of a new sector law, the establishment of an independent regulator, the gradual introduction of competition, the award of a second GSM license (for over \$1 billion), and the partial privatization of the incumbent.

Energy Statistics and Regional Benchmarking

Policy makers, donors, investors, and market participants need relevant, comprehensive, accurate, and timely energy sector statistics to make optimal decisions. Efficiency and performance indicators are especially important to identify bottlenecks and reform priorities, as well as to assess the impact of policy reforms through time-series analysis. To compare the performance of energy companies and the sector as a whole with those of other countries, harmonized data is needed for cross-country benchmarking. At present, however, energy statistics in the MPs are patchy, often outdated, unreliable, and compiled according to different methodologies. Performance and policy indicators (e.g. system losses, amount of subsidies, magnitude of arrears, rate of return, cost-recovery ratio) are particularly hard to come by. Official statistics rarely go beyond measuring production, consumption, and infrastructure endowments (e.g. generation capacity). Other structural problems include poor integration of national statistics offices on the one hand and energy authorities and utilities on the other; insufficient involvement of energy users and the private sector in the compilation of statistics (e.g. through user questionnaires); and a low level of transparency. During the research for this study, it became obvious that it is much easier to obtain sector statistics for the EU, Latin America, and Eastern Europe for instance, than for the MPs. One of the few exceptions in the region is Jordan. The annual report of the state utility NEPCO, for example, contains detailed statistics, performance indicators, and financial statements.

During the Granada Energy Forum, these problems were discussed and several country delegations asked the Commission to help improve sector statistics across the region. In fact, the three regional Meda projects "Reform of Legal, Regulatory, and Institutional Sector Frameworks", "Energy Company Restructuring", and "Support to the Three Ad-Hoc Groups" will all help to compile harmonized and detailed data on each of the MPs. This however, will require the close cooperation of national authorities and, in the longer run, institutional capacity building to improve the quality and availability of data. The Ad-Hoc Groups on Economic Analysis and Energy Policy are supposed to be used for those purposes. The consultants working on the regional Meda projects should make general data available through a website, to give all industry participants easy and timely access to relevant data. They should also take account of efforts to improve energy statistics within the EU, like EURELECTRIC's EURPROG database, statistical work done by the Commission's DG TREN and Eurostat, as well as a recent initiative by the Dutch and British authorities (DTI) to improve energy sector benchmarking within the EU.

Box 15:   The Southern African Power Pool

The Southern African Power Pool (SAPP), launched in 1995, was the first trans-national power pool in a developing region. It comprises a dozen countries with a total population of about 200 million people. The SAPP is legally based on an inter-governmental Memorandum of Understanding and subsidiary agreements, signed by participating governments and utilities. Institutional structures include a Technical and Administrative Unit (the secretariat), the Executive Committee (board of directors), and a Management Committee (administering the pool) with three sub-committees (for planning, operations, and environmental issues). A coordination center is responsible for pool monitoring, operation and planning studies, determination of transfer limits, management of a regional database, the coordination of maintenance schedules, and technical advise. SAPP is a *loose pool* without central dispatch. Members are obliged to have sufficient generation capacity, provide emergency energy for up to six hours, permit wheeling through their systems (transit rights), submit maintenance schedules, disclose information on generation cost structures, and contribute funds for the administration of the pool.

The Southern African Development Community (a regional grouping) and South Africa (as the dominant partner) were instrumental in mobilizing the political support needed to create the pool. A study had estimated possible cost savings to be as high as 20 percent. A number of policy lessons from the experience with the SAPP have been identified: (i) Power utilities in the member countries need to be commercialized and professionally managed to ensure that they respond to the commercial incentives of power trade and actively participate in the pool. (ii) Countries need to reach agreement on the mandate, design, and staffing of the coordination center as well as the establishment of effective dispute resolution procedures. (iii) Participation of a maximum number of power producers and customers is needed for sufficient liquidity within the pool. (iv) In order to ensure transparent and non-discriminatory access, all participating utilities should unbundle transmission, while rules for transmission pricing should be harmonized. (v) As member states reform their domestic power markets, full complementarity with the regulatory framework of the pool should be ensured.

Information taken from *Promoting Regional Power Trade – The Southern African Pool*, World Bank Viewpoint No. 145 (June 1998), by D. O'Leary et al (*www.worldbank.org/html/fpd/notes*)

4.3   Interconnections and Cross-Border Trade

Interconnections and the Mediterranean Electricity Ring

Most national grids within the region have been interconnected. Morocco is linked to the Spanish (and thus EU) grid and in 1999 entered a trial bid in the Spanish power pool. On the eastern side of the Mediterranean, an interconnection between Turkey (an MP) and Greece (an EU country) is under preparation. In the southern Mediterranean itself, most neighboring countries are already interconnected. The links between Morocco, Algeria, and Tunisia have been established and the interconnection between Tunisia and Libya is scheduled for completion in early 2001. In May 1998, the interconnector between Libya and Egypt was inaugurated and a year later the one between Egypt and Jordan, via the Gulf of Aqaba, came on stream. The links between Jordan and Syria and between Syria and Turkey are to be completed in late 2000.[61] In May 2000, the Arab Fund for Economic & Social Development agreed to provide a loan for the expansion of the interconnection between Lebanon and Syria. The most important remaining missing link is the one between Israel and its neighbors.

Once all these interconnections are completed, and their capacity has been sufficiently expanded, the Mediterranean Electricity Ring would be physically closed. Unlike EU markets, which are tightly interwoven, the Mediterranean Ring would constitute a "chain", which increases the interdependencies between the networks. The *regional Meda project "Mediterranean Electricity Ring"*, to be launched in late 2000, will analyze the technical and system management implications that this would entail (i.e. options for synchronization). Real market integration, however, will not only require physical interconnections and a stable, synchronized system, but also cross-border market liberalization and a harmonization of regulatory frameworks. There will be important interdependencies between national sector reforms, and the resolution of such cross-border issues. The *Ad-Hoc Group on Interconnection* (with the support it will receive from the Meda consultants from the regional project "Support to the Ad-Hoc Groups") should provide a forum to explore the economic potential and regulatory implications and opportunities arising from these interconnections.

Power Trade and Cross-Border Power Pools

Cross-border power trade enhances efficiency and can yield significant cost savings through (i) better emergency support; (ii) lower reserve margin requirements (i.e. lower investment needs and higher average capacity utilization); (iii) lower operating costs as a result of different load profiles; and (iv) increased competition. In the case of the MPs, emergency exchanges are already taking place. The potential for lower operating costs through complementary load profiles is likely to be limited. The most important benefits of increased power trade between the MPs are likely to come from the ability to lower reserve margins and from increased competition. In Jordan, for instance, it has been estimated that interconnections would permit the country to lower its reserve margins by 20 to 30 percent.[62] Particularly in the Middle East, many of the MPs have relatively small power markets and therefore effective competition in closed domestic markets is difficult to achieve without cross-border competition.

There are three basic models for international power markets. Under the *single buyer model*, a central entity purchases electricity from all producers and then resells it. This model, which does not necessarily require unbundling, limits competition. It is this model which currently exists throughout the region. The *open access (third-party) model* has more competitive trading mechanisms. Transmission systems are open to generators, who can sell directly to distributors or large customers. Most trades, however, continues to take place on the basis of long-term contracts. A precondition for such an arrangement is the effective regulation of network access,

---

[61] These interconnections and capacity increases are part of the "five country interconnection project" (Egypt, Jordan, Syria, Iraq and Turkey).

[62] MEED (22 May 1998)

63

and preferably the unbundling of transmission. In other words, functioning cross-border power markets require complementary domestic reforms. The third and most sophisticated type of trans-national power markets are *power pools*, or wholesale exchanges (see Section 2.4). Requirements for the operation of a pool are a well developed regulatory framework and institutional structures (e.g. spot and future markets, power traders) as well as a sufficiently large number of generators of similar size to permit effective competition.

Box 16:   The Baltic Sea Electricity Ring and Power Pool

One of the most interesting power markets currently emerging is the one around the Baltic Sea. Similar to the Mediterranean Electricity Ring, a *Baltic Ring* will connect the grid systems of EU member states and industrialized countries (Finland, Sweden, Norway, Denmark, and Germany) with those of transition economies (Russia, Estonia, Latvia, Lithuania, Belarus, and Poland). The two missing links that have to be completed are between Lithuania and Poland and between Estonia and Finland. At the country level, the Baltic states and Poland have started to comprehensively liberalize and privatize their electricity sectors in preparation of EU accession. At the regional level, a consensus is emerging that the construction of physical infrastructure is only one element in a strategy for market integration. Although the project is still at an early stage, it might become an interesting precedent for the Mediterranean Ring.

At a ministerial meeting in October 1999 in Helsinki, EU and Baltic energy ministers agreed to pursue the integration of energy markets throughout the region. The three Baltic countries Lithuania, Latvia, and Estonia are currently contemplating a four-stage plan, to be implemented over a seven-year period: the first stage would focus on open trade among them along the lines set out in the EU electricity directive; the second stage would implement full market integration with the EU; the third stage would be technical compliance with the UCTE standards governing Western European energy markets; and the fourth stage would involve the physical completion of the Baltic Ring. Access to Scandinavian markets would also create the option of joining Nord Pool (see also section 2.4).

A *Baltic Ring Study* has already analyzed most of the technical issues involved. Further cooperation is being pursued through *Baltrel*, which includes power companies and utility associations from eleven countries and 5 different grid systems. With financial assistance from the EC, it would analyze the status of systems and interconnections (both existing and planned) as well as legal and regulatory frameworks (e.g. grid codes); identify the obstacles to the development of open and competitive markets within the region; identify remedies to address them; and coordinate the implementation of agreed measures (including interconnection projects to complete the Baltic Ring). Regulatory reforms would include the harmonization of standards and regulations (e.g. unbundling of transmission, pricing mechanisms), the creation of a Baltrel Grid Code, and common operating rules. The creation of full-fledged power pool in the Baltic region over the coming decade seems to be a realistic scenario. The Euro-Med partners should follow the developments on the other side of the EU closely as they consider closing the Mediterranean Ring.

One of the central long-term objectives of the Euro-Mediterranean Energy Partnership should be the creation of more integrated and competitive regional power markets. Besides physical interconnection, this would require the modernization of the regulatory framework in the individual MPs (e.g. unbundling of transmission, open access, existence of similar size producers, commercialization of utilities). In addition, regional institutional and regulatory structures would have to be created in order to facilitate trade and create more competitive trans-national markets. According to one estimate, the economic benefits of electricity trade among the countries of North Africa alone could be as high as $ 200 million per year.[64] The instruments available for national reforms and the completion of the Mediterranean Ring are outlined above. The next step, in addition to these initiatives, would be the development of a strategy and an action plan for the creation of cross-border power markets. With sufficient political will, a regional market for electricity could theoretically be created within a decade; i.e. by the time the Euro-Mediterranean free-trade area is completed. The Southern African and the Baltic Power Pools (Box 15 and 16) could provide some interesting lessons.

Potential Sub-Regional Power Markets

Given the disparities and distances separating some MPs, there are cases where sub-regional cooperation should be considered. The emergence of regional trading hubs is also a feature of market dynamics within the EU single market. From an economic and efficiency point of view, grid connections and market integration would be particularly beneficial in the *Middle East*, with its many small systems. The only MPs currently not interconnected with their neighbors (but with each other) are Israel and the West Bank & Gaza. The physical and regulatory integration of Israel and its neighbors would not only permit the country to reduce its unusually high reserve margin, but could also significantly increase the competitiveness and efficiency of power markets in Jordan, the Palestine Territories, and Syria. As the Southern African energy pool and the recent agreement between Greece and Turkey shows, former adversaries can overcome political obstacles to reap the mutual economic benefits that interconnection and market integration can bring. Another potential sub-market could emerge between *Turkey, Greece, and Southeastern Europe*. In January 2000, an international consortium announced the intention to build a $ 500 million power station in southern Greece (the country's first private power plant), to supply the fast-growing Turkish market. The project is being backed by both governments.[65] A third sub-region that might lend itself to the creation of a more integrated power market is the *Maghreb*. The Ad-hoc Group on Interconnections and the consultants working on the regional Meda project for support of the three Ad-Hoc Groups should also explore the possibility of creating such sub-regional power markets.

---

[64] COMELEC has calculated that the cost savings from the reduced need for new generation capacity as a result of cross-border power trade between the Maghreb countries, for instance, would increase from $ 34 million in 2000 to $ 100 million in 2010.

[65] Financial Times (13 January 2000)

Box 17: The Energy Charter Treaty

The Energy Charter Treaty (ECT), which entered into force in April 1998, is a legally binding international agreement between currently 51 signatory countries (mainly from Europe, Central Asia, the Mediterranean). Based on the principles of market economy, mutual assistance, and non-discrimination, its aim is to promote energy cooperation and provide a stable framework for cross-border energy flows and investments. In principle, it covers all activities of the energy cycle (exploration, production, refining, transit, distribution, sale, efficient use) and all forms of energy (oil, gas, renewables, electricity). In practice, the ETC provisions are currently primarily relevant for the oil and gas sector but the possibility of adding an electricity protocol has been raised. The following excerpts, taken from the ECT website (*www.encharter.org*) outline *key elements of the Treaty:*

- *Secure Energy Investments* (Article 10):   Non-discrimination is the key principle. All foreign investments established in a host country are entitled to Most Favored Nation Treatment or National Treatment […] The contractual obligations between an investor and a host country must be respected. According to the Treaty's dispute resolution provision, a company or government can take a host government to international arbitration for a breach of contractual obligations. […] Host governments will allow foreign companies to transfer after-tax profits to any other country, without delay and in a freely convertible currency.

- *Facilitation of Trade* (Article 29):   Under the Treaty, GATT/WTO rules apply to all trades in energy materials and products where a non-WTO member is involved. For signatories that are not yet WTO members, the Treaty is an important step towards their WTO accession. The 1998 Trade Amendment updates the Treaty's trade regime to WTO rules and extends it to trade in energy-related equipment.

- *Freedom of Transit* (Article 7):   The Treaty is the first international agreement that establishes an elaborated multilateral transit framework for oil and gas pipelines and electricity grids. It contains a commitment to non-discrimination for use of facilities and transit conditions. […] In the event of a dispute over matters arising from transit […], a conciliator, appointed by the Secretary-General of the Energy Charter Secretariat, is to seek agreement of the Parties concerned, and may […] impose an interim tariff. […] The Treaty's provisions on transit are due to be strengthened through the adoption of an *Energy Charter Transit Protocol* [currently being negotiated] in recognition of the key importance of establishing a clearer regulatory framework among the Charter's states governing transit flows of energy, both hydrocarbons and electricity. [It should be noted, however, that this only concerns *transit* flows and that mandatory third-party access is explicitly excluded.] In parallel, a set of non-binding *Model Transit Agreements* is also being developed.

- *Effective Dispute Settlement for Investment* (Articles 26-28): The Treaty provides for international dispute settlement procedures that can be used between governments or investors. Both have the right to choose the form of international arbitration that best suits their needs.

- *Promoting Sustainable Development and Energy Efficiency* (Article 19):   The Energy Charter Treaty promotes internationally acknowledged standards for sustainable development—such as the 'polluter pays' principle and the practice of transparent environmental impact assessment. […] Contracting Parties shall promote market-oriented price formation and a fuller reflection of environmental costs and benefits […].

Participation of all MPs in the Energy Charter process is an important objective of the Euro-Mediterranean Energy Partnership. Cyprus is already a full member; Malta and Turkey have signed but not yet ratified the Treaty (a precondition for EU accession). Tunisia, Morocco, and Algeria have observer status at the Energy Charter Conference (the ECT's governing body). Ratification of the ECT could have several benefits for the MPs. It would send a political signal and give reassurance to potential investors. It would facilitate the construction of transit pipelines and interconnections. And it would be a step towards the harmonization of regulatory frameworks and energy market integration. In summary, the ETC can be a useful complement, but not a substitute for domestic reforms.

BIBLIOGRAPHY:

Energy Websites and Further Reading

Websites

- Association of European Transmission System Operators (ETSO): *www.etso-net.org*
- Association of Power Exchanges (APEX): *www.theapex.com*
- Competition law and regulation: *www.global-competition.com*
- Energy Charter Treaty: *www.encharter.org*
- Eurelectric: *www.eurelectric.org*
- European Commission: *www.europa.eu.int*
- European Commission, Directorate General for Energy and Transport (DG TREN): *www.europa.eu.int/comm/dgs/energy_transport/index_en.html* [information on EU legislation, energy markets, and Commission activities in the energy sector]
- European Federation of Energy Traders (EFET): *www.efet.org*
- International Energy Agency: *www.iea.org*
- Middle East Economic Digest (MEED): *www.meed.com* [weekly news about the region, including developments in the energy sector]
- National Economic Research Associates (NERA): *www.nera.com* [very detailed and comprehensive monthly newsletter on Global Energy Regulation]
- Office of Gas and Electricity Markets (OFGEM), UK: *www.ofgem.gov.uk*
- Power in East Europe and East European Energy Report: *www.ftenergy.com* [two periodicals about the energy sector in Eastern Europe]
- Sustainable Minnesota: *www.me3.org/projects/dereg/nonmn.html* [web-links and documents concerning power sector reform in the United States]
- U.S. Department of Energy, Country Analysis Briefs for the Energy Sector: *www.eia.doe.gov*
- Union for the Coordination of Transmission of Electricity (UCTE): *www.ucte.org*
- World Bank: *www.worldbank.org*

Documents   [Documents marked with "@" can be downloaded from above sites. World Bank Viewpoints are posted at: *www. worldbank.org/html/fpd/notes/*]

Energy Reform

- *Private Participation in Energy – Global Trends*, World Bank Viewpoint No. 208 (May 2000), by A. K. Izaguirre @
- *A Scorecard for Energy Reform in the Developing Countries*, World Bank Viewpoint No. 175 (April 1999), by R. Bacon @
- *Reshaping Power Markets – Lessons from Chile and Argentina*, World Bank Viewpoint No. 85 (June 1996), by P. Lalor and H. García @
- *Privatization of the Power and Natural Gas Industries in Hungary and Kazakhstan*, World Bank Technical Paper No. 451 (1999), 140 pages
- *Towards Unbundling in the EU Electricity Industry*, Eurelectric (1999) [The report explains some of the implications of unbundling for utility management and can be downloaded from the Eurelectric website] @
- *Electricity Market Reform—An IEA Handbook*, International Energy Agency (February 1999)
- *Appropriate Restructuring Strategies for the Power Generation Sector—The Case of Small Systems*, World Bank (1995), by Robert Bacon [good overview over key sector issues]

- *The Euro-Mediterranean Energy Partnership*, Financial Times Energy, by Debra Johnson, (June 2000) [The book can be regarded as complementary to this publication: (i) It focuses more on hydrocarbons, while this publication is primarily concerned with electricity. (ii) The FT book describes stocks and flows of energy, as well as specific projects; whereas this one analyses sector policies. (iii) The main audience of former is the private sector, the one of latter are governments and donors.]
- *Key Issues and Lessons Learned from the Electricity Sector Reforms in Latin America*, prepared for the Interamerican Development Bank and the United States Agency for International Development by Hagler Bailly Services (1999) [not published]

IPPs and Concessions

- *Private Participation in Energy*, World Bank Viewpoint No. 208 (May 2000), by A. K. Izaguirre [A good discussion of Asia's negative experience with IPPs on page 6.] @
- *The Impact of IPPs in Developing Countries – Out of the Crisis and into the Future*, World Bank Viewpoint No. 162 (December 1998), by Y. Albouy and R. Bousba @
- *Regulatory Lessons from Argentine's Power Concessions*, World Bank Viewpoint No. 92 (September 1996), by A. Estache and M. Rodriguez-Pardina @
- *The Privatization Challenge*, World Bank Regional and Sectoral Studies, by P. Guislain (1997), 399 pages [A cross-sector overview of policy issues and best practice in privatization.]
- *Concessions for Infrastructure – A Guide to Their Design and Award*, World Bank Technical Paper No. 399, by M. Kerf et al (March 1998), 120 pages
- *Bidding for Concessions – The Impact of Contract Design*, Viewpoint No. 158 (November 1998), World Bank Viewpoint No. 158, by M. Klein @
- *Contingent Liabilities for Infrastructure Projects – Implementing a Risk Management Framework for Governments*, World Bank Viewpoint No. 148 (August 1998), by C. Lewis & A. Mody @
- *Best Practice in Power Sector Privatization in Central and Eastern Europe*, United States Energy Association (USEA) and United States Agency for International Development (USAID), January 2001, @ (at *www.usea.org*)

Cross-Border Trade and Power Pools

- *Promoting Regional Power Trade – The Southern African Power Pool*, World Bank Viewpoint No. 145 (June 1998), by D. O'Leary et al @
- *International Power Trade – The Nordic Power Pool*, World Bank Viewpoint No. 171 (January 1999), by L. Carlsson @
- *Developing International Power Markets in East Asia*, World Bank Viewpoint No. 143 (May 1998), by E. Crousillat [includes good overview over different types of power trade] @
- *International Power Connections – Moving from Electricity Exchange to Competitive Trade*, World Bank Viewpoint No. 42 (March 1995), by J. Charpentier and K. Schenk @
- *Baltic Ring Study* (*www.balticring.com/html/study.htm*) @

Natural Gas Markets

- *Natural Gas – Private Sector Participation and Market Development*, World Bank (1999) [A bound collection of Viewpoint case-studies, some of which listed below (95 pages)]
- *Private Participation in the Transmission and Distribution of Natural Gas – Recent Trends*, World Bank Viewpoint No. 176 (April 1999), by A. K. Izaguirre @
- *Regulation in New Natural Gas Markets – The Northern Ireland Experience*, World Bank Viewpoint No. 179 (April 1998), by P. Lehmann @

- *International Gas Trade – The Bolivia-Brazil Gas Pipeline*, World Bank Viewpoint # 144 (May 1998), by P. Law and N. de Franco @
- *Competition in the Natural Gas Industry – The Emergence of Spot, Financial, and Pipeline Capacity Markets*, World Bank Viewpoint No. 137 (March 1998), by A. Juris @
- *North African & Mediterranean Gas*, Emerging Markets (*www.emerging-markets.com*) @

Regulation

- *Utility Regulators – Supporting Nascent Institutions in the Developing World*, World Bank Viewpoint No. 153 (September 1998), by P. Gray @
- *Utility Regulators – Decisionmaking Structures, Resources, and Start-up Strategy*, World Bank Viewpoint No. 129 (September 1997), by W. Smith @
- *Utility Regulators – Roles and Responsibilities*, World Bank Viewpoint No. 128 (September 1998), by W. Smith @
- *Utility Regulators – The Independence Debate*, World Bank Viewpoint No. 127 (September 1997), by W. Smith @
- *Governance and Regulation of Power Pools and System Operators – An International Comparison*, World Bank Technical Paper No. 382 (September 1997), by J. Barker et al

Environment, Social Issues, and Government Subsidies

- *Market-Based Instruments for Environmental Policy Making in Latin America and the Caribbean – Lessons from Eleven Countries*, World Bank Discussion Paper No. 381 (November 1998), by R. Huber et al
- *Financial Incentives for Renewable Energy Development – Proceedings from an International Workshop*, World Bank Discussion Paper No. 391 (October 1998), by S. Piscitello and S. Bogach
- *Price Structures, Cross-Subsidies, and Competition in Infrastructure*, World Bank Viewpoint No. 107 (February 1997), by T. Irwin @
- *Auctioning Subsidies for Rural Electrification in Chile*, World Bank Viewpoint No. 214 (June 2000), by A. Jadresic @
- *The Costs of Corruption for the Poor – The Energy Sector*, World Bank Viewpoint No. 207 (April 2000), by L. Lovei and A. McKechnie @
- *Power Theft: An Insidious Menace*, Power Economics (July 1999), by D. Appleyard

Distributors of World Bank Group Publications

Prices and credit terms vary from country to country. Consult your local distributor before placing an order.

ARGENTINA
World Publications SA
Av. Cordoba 1877
1120 Ciudad de Buenos Aires
Tel: (54 11) 4815-8156
Fax: (54 11) 4815-8156
E-mail: wpbooks@infovia.com.ar

AUSTRALIA, FIJI, PAPUA NEW GUINEA, SOLOMON ISLANDS, VANUATU, AND SAMOA
D.A. Information Services
648 Whitehorse Road
Mitcham 3132, Victoria
Tel: (61) 3 9210 7777
Fax: (61) 3 9210 7788
E-mail: service@dadirect.com.au
URL: http://www.dadirect.com.au

AUSTRIA
Gerold and Co.
Weihburggasse 26
A-1011 Wien
Tel: (43 1) 512-47-31-0
Fax: (43 1) 512-47-31-29
URL: http://www.gerold.co/at.online

BANGLADESH
Micro Industries Development
Assistance Society (MIDAS)
House 5, Road 16
Dhanmondi R/Area
Dhaka 1209
Tel: (880 2) 326427
Fax: (880 2) 811188

BELGIUM
Jean De Lannoy
Av. du Roi 202
1060 Brussels
Tel: (32 2) 538-5169
Fax: (32 2) 538-0841

BRAZIL
Publicaçőes Tecnicas Internacionais
Ltda.
Rua Peixoto Gomide, 209
01409 Sao Paulo, SP.
Tel: (55 11) 259-6644
Fax: (55 11) 258-6990
E-mail: postmaster@pti.uol.br
URL: http://www.uol.br

CANADA
Renouf Publishing Co. Ltd.
5369 Canotek Road
Ottawa, Ontario K1J 9J3
Tel: (613) 745-2665
Fax: (613) 745-7660
E-mail: order.dept@renoufbooks.com
URL: http://www.renoufbooks.com

CHINA
China Financial & Economic
Publishing House
8, Da Fo Si Dong Jie
Beijing
Tel: (86 10) 6401-7365
Fax: (86 10) 6401-7365

China Book Import Centre
P.O. Box 2825
Beijing

Chinese Corporation for Promotion of Humanities
52, You Fang Hu Tong,
Xuan Nei Da Jie
Beijing
Tel: (86 10) 660 72 494
Fax: (86 10) 660 72 494

COLOMBIA
Infoenlace Ltda.
Carrera 6 No. 51-21
Apartado Aereo 34270
Santafé de Bogotá, D.C.
Tel: (57 1) 285-2798
Fax: (57 1) 285-2798

COTE D'IVOIRE
Center d'Edition et de Diffusion
Africaines (CEDA)
04 B.P. 541
Abidjan 04
Tel: (225) 24 6510; 24 6511
Fax: (225) 25 0567

CYPRUS
Center for Applied Research
Cyprus College
6, Diogenes Street, Engomi
P.O. Box 2006
Nicosia
Tel: (357 2) 59-0730
Fax: (357 2) 66-2051

CZECH REPUBLIC
USIS, NIS Prodejna
Havelkova 22
130 00 Prague 3
Tel: (420 2) 2423 1486
Fax: (420 2) 2423 1114
URL: http://www.nis.cz/

DENMARK
SamfundsLitteratur
Rosenoerns Allé 11
DK-1970 Frederiksberg C
Tel: (45 35) 351942
Fax: (45 35) 357822
URL: http://www.si.cbs.dk

ECUADOR
Libri Mundi
Libreria Internacional
P.O. Box 17-01-3029
Juan Leon Mera 851
Quito
Tel: (593 2) 521-606; (593 2) 544-185
Fax: (593 2) 504-209
E-mail: librimu1@librimundi.com.ec
E-mail: librimu2@librimundi.com.ec

CODEU
Ruiz de Castilla 763, Edif. Expocolor
Primer piso, Of. #2
Quito
Tel/Fax: (593 2) 507-383; 253-091
E-mail: codeu@impsat.net.ec

EGYPT, ARAB REPUBLIC OF
Al Ahram Distribution Agency
Al Galaa Street
Cairo
Tel: (20 2) 578-6083
Fax: (20 2) 578-6833

The Middle East Observer
41, Sherif Street
Cairo
Tel: (20 2) 393-9732
Fax: (20 2) 393-9732

FINLAND
Akateeminen Kirjakauppa
P.O. Box 128
FIN-00101 Helsinki
Tel: (358 0) 121 4418
Fax: (358 0) 121-4435
E-mail: akatilaus@stockmann.fi
URL: http://www.akateeminen.com

FRANCE
Editions Eska; DBJ
48, rue Gay Lussac
75005 Paris
Tel: (33-1) 55-42-73-08
Fax: (33-1) 43-29-91-67

GERMANY
UNO-Verlag
Poppelsdorfer Allee 55
53115 Bonn
Tel: (49 228) 949020
Fax: (49 228) 217492
URL: http://www.uno-verlag.de
E-mail: unoverlag@aol.com

GHANA
Epp Books Services
P.O. Box 44
TUC
Accra
Tel: 223 21 778843
Fax: 223 21 779099

GREECE
Papasotiriou S.A.
35, Stournara Str.
106 82 Athens
Tel: (30 1) 364-1826
Fax: (30 1) 364-8254

HAITI
Culture Diffusion
5, Rue Capois
C.P. 257
Port-au-Prince
Tel: (509) 23 9260
Fax: (509) 23 4858

HONG KONG, CHINA; MACAO
Asia 2000 Ltd.
Sales & Circulation Department
302 Seabird House
22-28 Wyndham Street, Central
Hong Kong, China
Tel: (852) 2530-1409
Fax: (852) 2526-1107
E-mail: sales@asia2000.com.hk
URL: http://www.asia2000.com.hk

HUNGARY
Euro Info Service
Margitszgeti Europa Haz
H-1138 Budapest
Tel: (36 1) 350 80 24, 350 80 25
Fax: (36 1) 350 90 32
E-mail: euroinfo@mail.matav.hu

INDIA
Allied Publishers Ltd.
751 Mount Road
Madras - 600 002
Tel: (91 44) 852-3938
Fax: (91 44) 852-0649

INDONESIA
Pt. Indira Limited
Jalan Borobudur 20
P.O. Box 181
Jakarta 10320
Tel: (62 21) 390-4290
Fax: (62 21) 390-4289

IRAN
Ketab Sara Co. Publishers
Khaled Eslamboli Ave., 6th Street
Delafrooz Alley No. 8
P.O. Box 15745-733
Tehran 15117
Tel: (98 21) 8717819; 8716104
Fax: (98 21) 8712479
E-mail: ketab-sara@neda.net.ir

Kowkab Publishers
P.O. Box 19575-511
Tehran
Tel: (98 21) 258-3723
Fax: (98 21) 258-3723

IRELAND
Government Supplies Agency
Oifig an tSoláthair
4-5 Harcourt Road
Dublin 2
Tel: (353 1) 661-3111
Fax: (353 1) 475-2670

ISRAEL
Yozmot Literature Ltd.
P.O. Box 56055
3 Yohanan Hasandlar Street
Tel Aviv 61560
Tel: (972 3) 5285-397
Fax: (972 3) 5285-397

R.O.Y. International
PO Box 13056
Tel Aviv 61130
Tel: (972 3) 649 9469
Fax: (972 3) 648 6039
E-mail: royil@netvision.net.il
URL: http://www.royint.co.il

Palestinian Authority/Middle East
Index Information Services
P.O.B. 19502 Jerusalem
Tel: (972 2) 6271219
Fax: (972 2) 6271634

ITALY, LIBERIA
Licosa Commissionaria Sansoni SPA
Via Duca Di Calabria, 1/1
Casella Postale 552
50125 Firenze
Tel: (39 55) 645-415
Fax: (39 55) 641-257
E-mail: licosa@ftbcc.it
URL: http://www.ftbcc.it/licosa

JAMAICA
Ian Randle Publishers Ltd.
206 Old Hope Road, Kingston 6
Tel: 876-927-2085
Fax: 876-977-0243
E-mail: irpl@colis.com

JAPAN
Eastern Book Service
3-13 Hongo 3-chome, Bunkyo-ku
Tokyo 113
Tel: (81 3) 3818-0861
Fax: (81 3) 3818-0864
E-mail: orders@svt-ebs.co.jp
URL:
http://www.bekkoame.or.jp/~svt-ebs

KENYA
Africa Book Service (E.A.) Ltd.
Quaran House, Mfangano Street
P.O. Box 45245
Nairobi
Tel: (254 2) 223 641
Fax: (254 2) 330 272

Legacy Books
Loita House
Mezzanine 1
P.O. Box 68077
Nairobi
Tel: (254) 2-330853, 221426
Fax: (254) 2-330854, 561654
E-mail: Legacy@form-net.com

KOREA, REPUBLIC OF
Dayang Books Trading Co.
International Division
783-20, Pangba Bon-Dong,
Socho-ku
Seoul
Tel: (82 2) 536-9555
Fax: (82 2) 536-0025
E-mail: seamap@chollian.net

Eulyoo Publishing Co., Ltd.
46-1, Susong-Dong
Jongro-Gu
Seoul
Tel: (82 2) 734-3515
Fax: (82 2) 732-9154

LEBANON
Librairie du Liban
P.O. Box 11-9232
Beirut
Tel: (961 9) 217 944
Fax: (961 9) 217 434
E-mail: hsayegh@librairie-du-liban.com.lb
URL: http://www.librairie-du-liban.com.lb

MALAYSIA
University of Malaya Cooperative
Bookshop, Limited
P.O. Box 1127
Jalan Pantai Baru
59700 Kuala Lumpur
Tel: (60 3) 756-5000
Fax: (60 3) 755-4424
E-mail: umkoop@tm.net.my

MEXICO
INFOTEC
Av. San Fernando No. 37
Col. Toriello Guerra
14050 Mexico, D.F.
Tel: (52 5) 624-2800
Fax: (52 5) 624-2822
E-mail: infotec@rtn.net.mx
URL: http://rtn.net.mx

Mundi-Prensa Mexico S.A. de C.V.
c/Rio Panuco, 141-Colonia
Cuauhtemoc
06500 Mexico, D.F.
Tel: (52 5) 533-5658
Fax: (52 5) 514-6799

NEPAL
Everest Media International Services
(P.) Ltd.
GPO Box 5443
Kathmandu
Tel: (977 1) 416 026
Fax: (977 1) 224 431

NETHERLANDS
De Lindeboom/Internationale
Publicaties b.v.-
P.O. Box 202, 7480 AE Haaksbergen
Tel: (31 53) 574-0004
Fax: (31 53) 572-9296
E-mail: lindeboo@worldonline.nl
URL: http://www.worldonline.nl/~lindeboo

NEW ZEALAND
EBSCO NZ Ltd.
Private Mail Bag 99914
New Market
Auckland
Tel: (64 9) 524-8119
Fax: (64 9) 524-8067

Oasis Official
P.O. Box 3627
Wellington
Tel: (64 4) 499 1551
Fax: (64 4) 499 1972
E-mail: oasis@actrix.gen.nz
URL: http://www.oasisbooks.co.nz/

NIGERIA
University Press Limited
Three Crowns Building Jericho
Private Mail Bag 5095
Ibadan
Tel: (234 22) 41-1356
Fax: (234 22) 41-2056

PAKISTAN
Mirza Book Agency
65, Shahrah-e-Quaid-e-Azam
Lahore 54000
Tel: (92 42) 735 3601
Fax: (92 42) 576 3714

Oxford University Press
5 Bangalore Town
Sharae Faisal
PO Box 13033
Karachi-75350
Tel: (92 21) 446307
Fax: (92 21) 4547640
E-mail: ouppak@TheOffice.net

Pak Book Corporation
Aziz Chambers 21, Queen's Road
Lahore
Tel: (92 42) 636 3222; 636 0885
Fax: (92 42) 636 2328
E-mail: pbc@brain.net.pk

PERU
Editorial Desarrollo SA
Apartado 3824, Ica 242 OF. 106
Lima 1
Tel: (51 14) 285380
Fax: (51 14) 286628

PHILIPPINES
International Booksource Center Inc.
1127-A Antipolo St, Barangay,
Venezuela
Makati City
Tel: (63 2) 896 6501; 6505; 6507
Fax: (63 2) 896 1741

POLAND
International Publishing Service
Ul. Piekna 31/37
00-677 Warzawa
Tel: (48 2) 628-6089
Fax: (48 2) 621-7255
E-mail: books%ips@ikp.atm.com.pl
URL: http://www.ipscg.waw.pl/ips/export

PORTUGAL
Livraria Portugal
Apartado 2681, Rua Do Carm
o 70-74
1200 Lisbon
Tel: (1) 347-4982
Fax: (1) 347-0264

ROMANIA
Compani De Librarii Bucuresti S.A.
Str. Lipscani no. 26, sector 3
Bucharest
Tel: (40 1) 313 9645
Fax: (40 1) 312 4000

RUSSIAN FEDERATION
Isdatelstvo <Ves Mir>
9a, Kolpachniy Pereulok
Moscow 101831
Tel: (7 095) 917 87 49
Fax: (7 095) 917 92 59
ozimarin@glasnet.ru

SINGAPORE; TAIWAN, CHINA MYANMAR; BRUNEI
Hemisphere Publication Services
41 Kallang Pudding Road #04-03
Golden Wheel Building
Singapore 349316
Tel: (65) 741-5166
Fax: (65) 742-9356
E-mail: ashgate@asianconnect.com

SLOVENIA
Gospodarski vestnik Publishing
Group
Dunajska cesta 5
1000 Ljubljana
Tel: (386 61) 133 83 47; 132 12 30
Fax: (386 61) 133 80 30
E-mail: repansekj@gvestnik.si

SOUTH AFRICA, BOTSWANA
For single titles:
Oxford University Press Southern
Africa
Vasco Boulevard, Goodwood
P.O. Box 12119, N1 City 7463
Cape Town
Tel: (27 21) 595 4400
Fax: (27 21) 595 4430
E-mail: oxford@oup.co.za

For subscription orders:
International Subscription Service
P.O. Box 41095
Craighall
Johannesburg 2024
Tel: (27 11) 880-1448
Fax: (27 11) 880-6248
E-mail: iss@is.co.za

SPAIN
Mundi-Prensa Libros, S.A.
Castello 37
28001 Madrid
Tel: (34 91) 4 363700
Fax: (34 91) 5 753998
E-mail: libreria@mundiprensa.es
URL: http://www.mundiprensa.com/

Mundi-Prensa Barcelona
Conseil de Cent, 391
08009 Barcelona
Tel: (34 3) 488-3492
Fax: (34 3) 487-7659
E-mail: barcelona@mundiprensa.es

SRI LANKA, THE MALDIVES
Lake House Bookshop
100, Sir Chittampalam Gardiner
Mawatha
Colombo 2
Tel: (94 1) 32105
Fax: (94 1) 432104
E-mail: LHL@sri.lanka.net

SWEDEN
Wennergren-Williams AB
P. O. Box 1305
S-171 25 Solna
Tel: (46 8) 705-97-50
Fax: (46 8) 27-00-71
E-mail: mail@wwi.se

SWITZERLAND
Librairie Payot Service Institutionnel
C(tm)tes-de-Montbenon 30
1002 Lausanne
Tel: (41 21) 341-3229
Fax: (41 21) 341-3235

ADECO Van Diermen
EditionsTechniques
Ch. de Lacuez 41
CH1807 Blonay
Tel: (41 21) 943 2673
Fax: (41 21) 943 3605

THAILAND
Central Books Distribution
306 Silom Road
Bangkok 10500
Tel: (66 2) 2336930-9
Fax: (66 2) 237-8321

TRINIDAD & TOBAGO AND THE CARRIBBEAN
Systematics Studies Ltd.
St. Augustine Shopping Center
Eastern Main Road, St. Augustine
Trinidad & Tobago, West Indies
Tel: (868) 645-8466
Fax: (868) 645-8467
E-mail: tobe@trinidad.net

UGANDA
Gustro Ltd.
PO Box 9997, Madhvani Building
Plot 16/4 Jinja Rd.
Kampala
Tel: (256 41) 251 467
Fax: (256 41) 251 468
E-mail: gus@swiftuganda.com

UNITED KINGDOM
Microinfo Ltd.
P.O. Box 3, Omega Park, Alton,
Hampshire GU34 2PG
England
Tel: (44 1420) 86848
Fax: (44 1420) 89889
E-mail: wbank@microinfo.co.uk
URL: http://www.microinfo.co.uk

The Stationery Office
51 Nine Elms Lane
London SW8 5DR
Tel: (44 171) 873-8400
Fax: (44 171) 873-8242
URL: http://www.the-stationery-office.co.uk/

VENEZUELA
Tecni-Ciencia Libros, S.A.
Centro Cuidad Comercial Tamanco
Nivel C2, Caracas
Tel: (58 2) 959 5547; 5035; 0016
Fax: (58 2) 959 5636

ZAMBIA
University Bookshop, University of
Zambia
Great East Road Campus
P.O. Box 32379
Lusaka
Tel: (260 1) 252 576
Fax: (260 1) 253 952

ZIMBABWE
Academic and Baobab Books (Pvt.)
Ltd.
4 Conald Road, Graniteside
P.O. Box 567
Harare
Tel: 263 4 755035
Fax: 263 4 781913

www.ingramcontent.com/pod-product-compliance
Lightning Source LLC
Chambersburg PA
CBHW081200270326
41930CB00014B/3231